Charles Welsh Mason

Poems and Songs of Which Some are Rendered from the Spanish

Charles Welsh Mason

Poems and Songs of Which Some are Rendered from the Spanish

ISBN/EAN: 9783744775816

Printed in Europe, USA, Canada, Australia, Japan

Cover: Foto ©Thomas Meinert / pixelio.de

More available books at **www.hansebooks.com**

POEMS AND SONGS

OF WHICH SOME ARE RENDERED

FROM THE SPANISH.

BY

CHARLES WELSH MASON.

LONDON: BELL AND DALDY.
CAMBRIDGE: DEIGHTON, BELL, AND CO.
1863.

Cambridge:
PRINTED BY JONATHAN PALMER.

Dedicated

BY PERMISSION

TO

LORD HOUGHTON.

CONTENTS.

	Page
A MONODY ON THE DEATH OF THE LATE PRINCE CONSORT	1
IMITATIONS AND TRANSLATIONS FROM THE SPANISH	34
ENGLISH LYRICS	55

A MONODY

ON THE DEATH OF

THE LATE PRINCE CONSORT.

"He, onely, like himselfe, was second unto none,
Whose deth (through life) we rue, and al in vain do mone."

PART I.

I.

WHAT shall I say, to whom the past
  Is present still? What sing of Death,
  Who taketh naught away but breath,
Who leaveth naught which shall not last?

Who leaveth love, a little spark
  Half quench'd in tears which flow amain;
  Who leaveth, through the night of pain,
A beacon, burning in the dark.

II.

To us the past appeareth sad,
    Who feel our loss, but cannot see
    His gain, or ours; which seeing, He,
For us and for himself, is glad.

And greater than our loss, I ween
    Loss could not be: for thine, sweet soul,
    Is ours, who seemest, in thy dole,
Crown'd with our sorrow, sorrow's Queen.

And deeper than the constant sea
    Which maketh moan upon the shore,
    Our love doth grow to more and more,
And with its arms encompass thee.

III.

To us the past is present still,
 Who linger in the tearful vale;
 Who court not any changeful gale
Which wantons on the breezy hill.

To Her, to us, the vale is dear,
 The sweet sad past which passeth not:
 We mourn around a mournful spot,
We languish for a by-gone year.

And still among us lives his name,
 The man with head, and heart, and hand;
 And all about the sorrowing land,
From lip to lip is breathed his fame.

PART II.

I.

What art Thou, having past away,
    Clear head, great heart, and royal hand?
    Doth thy consummate spirit stand,
Among our spirits, here, to-day?

What seëst Thou, whose eyes are free
    From mortal blindness? Let us know
    The dead are round us. Let us grow
To that which Thou would'st have us be.

II.

O CLEAR in thought, and pure in heart!
    What tribute shall we bring to Thee,
    Who brookest no impurity,
Who knowest now, no more in part?

Who seëst from a blissful clime
    That which we seek among the years,
    And falter, blinded with our tears,
And lost among the mists of time.

No thought or act we offer Thee:
    A crown of love with tears we bring
    To Her, and in the song we sing
A sigh for purer love to be.

III.

With close-lock'd hands, and mingled tears,
    We linger in the valley still;
    And round the bases of the hill
A mist is driven from the meres.

From out the mist come feeble cries,
    Which mingle madly right with wrong.
    We only know that Thou art strong,
And holdest truth among the wise:

Great Death hath made thee wise and strong:
    Our loss is dearer for Thy gain:
    And growing wise in bearing pain,
We learn to sunder right from wrong.

PART III.

I.

What shall I sing of Death who came,
    An angel robed in white, and bore
    Him from us weeping on the shore?
How shall I measure praise or blame?

O Death! Thou seëst how we mourn.
    We doubt not, but our eyes are dim;
    We fain would have a glimpse of Him
In that still place, beyond the bourne.

And, waiting by with folded wing,
    The angel answers, "Be content:
    Ye draw towards a great event,
Not seeing what the seasons bring."

II.

Beyond the bourne we have not been,
    And he who goes may not return;
    Or, coming back, we may not learn
What are the things which he has seen.

And even Him we may not see.
    The silent Soul is with us still,
    Contèmplating our little ill
In that great light which is to be.

We may not see: we can but trust
    That He hath seen the end of all,
    Discerneth that we shall not fall
Although we falter in the dust.

PART IV.

I.

The bells of Yule ring out again
 The dying year. With note of woe,
 And clang of war, the seasons go;
And Thou art gone, but we remain.

The seasons go, and swiftly come
 The sister-seasons in their train;
 They come and go, but we, in pain,
Await a passage to our home;

Nor sit and sing, with idle hand,
 But mingle in the toil and strife,
 And battle with the surge of life
Upon the borders of the land.

II.

But ever sweet it seems to dream
    Of Him we loved, at dewy dawn,
    Or when long shadows span the lawn
And lie athwart the rosy stream.

And memory mingles other days
    With those which are, and solace brings
    To one who tunes his harp, and sings
Of grief that goes and love that stays;

Of love that cannot pass away,
    Though all things else may come and go,
    And life shall languish, as the snow
Which fails before a summer day.

PART V.

I.

What shall I sing of Death? who came,
    A silent messenger of LOVE,
    And led Him to the courts above
Who bore on earth a splendid name,

Who wore his splendour without pride,
    Who nobly fill'd a royal part,
    A prince in deed, a king in heart,
Meet Consort for a peerless Bride.

The form shall moulder in the grave:
    Thus much was fashion'd out of dust,
    And we, though sad to lose it, must
Return to earth the gift she gave.

To Nature we resign the form,
    Well knowing that she will not lose
    An atom, though the wild wind blows,
And ever beats the pitiless storm.

II.

With unremitting toil, the wave
    Wears out the old sepulchral rock.
    Hereafter mighty throes will shock
The crust of earth that holds thy grave:

For peopled town, and lonely grange,
    Fair flower'd dell, and forest-trees,
    Shall mingle under rolling seas,
And all that is shall suffer change.

Old races perish. But a few
    Faint tracks remain. New forms abound
    A little while, then strew the ground;
But over all the eternal blue.

Here seemeth tumult, jar and strife,
    New forms and types replacing all,
    A birth and death, a rise and fall,
But thence a voice, "I am the Life."

III.

AND through the seeming tumult, Thou
    Did'st see the unseen, beyond the strife
    Which throngs the crowded ways of life;
Then seeing darkly, clearly now;

For ever with the True and Just,
    In whom we live and blindly move,
    In weakness leaning on the love
Which summon'd Nature out of dust,

And gave to her the changeful Hours
    Which in a circle round her stand,
    And gave to Death the border-land
Which lies between thy soul and ours.

IV.

FEEBLY we go in darkness here,
    With failing heart and aching brain.
    Sad billows murmur on the main,
'O that the end, the end were near!'

'What end?' I answer, making moan,
    'The end, the end,' they murmur still;
    And rocks the myriad-vaulted hill;
And all the weary seasons groan.

Redeeméd Soul, I would not vex
    Thy wisdom with a foolish song.
    Sweet Nature do'th not any wrong,
Though all her ways my soul perplex.

We cleave to faith, we watch and pray,
    We fold thy mantle round the heart,
    And watching, as we sit apart,
Catch distant glimpses of the day.

PART VI.

I.

Pure was thy life, and fair thy death,
    A perfect lesson Thou hast left,
    Which he may learn who is bereft,
Or in disquiet wandereth:

Allegiance to the true and good,
    A constant heart, an eye that saw
    God's ordinance in human law,
A little raft upon the flood:

A life fulfill'd with noble deeds,
    A simple manly chastity,
    A soul where rested charity
Above the tumult of the creeds.

II.

I WEEP for Her, my grief is theirs
    Who knew Thee most and loved Thee best:
    We sadden, but there cometh rest,
An after-fruit of tears and prayers;

And LOVE abideth evermore
    To Thee, to us, and over all.
    O Death, we come if thou but call;
We yearn to quit the doubtful shore.

III.

O LOVE, who art and wilt endure,
　　Great Nature circles at Thy feet:
　　In Thee, at length, we trust to meet,
When Thou hast made our passion pure.

FROM THE SPANISH.

ZAIDÉ.

"Tuya soy, tuya seré
Y tuya es mi vida, Zaidé."

I.

PACING in a narrow street,
    For a footfall listening,
For the light fall of light feet
In a balconied retreat,
Where long tendrils droop and meet,
    While the stars are glistening;

II.

Pacing moodily below,
    Groaning in his sorrow,
Vext with bitter pang and throe,
Vext at one delaying so,
While the weary hours go
    Creeping towards the morrow;

III.

In upon his clouded heart
    Steals a ray of gladness,
Making all the gloom depart,
Felt in darkness when apart,
Healing all the ancient smart,
    Cheering all his sadness;

IV.

In among the dew-dript flowers
    Drowsily awaking,
On the floor of terraced bowers
Drops a foot-fall, like soft showers
Kissing leaves in April hours,
    While the dawn is breaking;

V.

Comes a vision past compare
    Of a maiden slender,
Mantled with a veil of hair,
Draped in linen pure and fair,
While the Moor stands gazing there,
    Rapt in musings tender.

VI.

'*Bella Mora!* Slender maid!
    Silent is my pleading;
Not a sound of serenade,
Not a ring of spur or blade,
Not a murmur in the shade,
    Tho' my heart is bleeding.'

VII.

'*A te Moro!* Alá knows
    My heart too is wailing,
Woeful at the coming close
Of its blissful dream, which goes,
Like fair upland veil of snows
    In the bright sun failing.'

VIII.

'Let thy fair dream fail and go,
    Fairer dawns the morrow;
Shall thy tears like fountains flow
Night and day? Dear love, not so:
Lose thy fears, and trusting, know
    Loss of all thy sorrow.'

IX.

Quail'd she then at love's behest,
　　Doubtful blushes hiding.
'Ere the night fail'd in the west,
Drooping on her lover's breast,
Found she there true maiden's rest
　　In love's strength abiding.

ROMANCES MORISCOS.

CANCION.

" De ver-le penar asi
Muy penada vivo yo,
Y remedio no le do.

More than little he loves me,
More than who should kinder be,
Loves me for this cruelty.

Yet, in being cruel to him,
My frail heart is rent with woe:
My vext eyes with tears grow dim,
Tears that rise but will not flow,
Seeing that he suffers so:
Shall I own it? No, ah no!

CRISTÓBAL DE CASTILLÉJO.

XARIFA. 1.

"*Peynaba yo mis cabellos*
Con cuidado cada dia,
Y el viento los esparzia
Robando-me los mas bellos,
Ya su soplo y sombra d'ellos
Mi querido se durmio,
Si le recordare? O no!"

PRIMAVERA DE VARIOS ROMANCES, p. 88.

I.

At morn I leave
My couch, and fondly comb my golden hair:
Of leaf and bud I weave
A chaplet rare,
Wherewith to make
My fair brow fairer at the noontide hour,
For thy sweet sake,
And to my sweetness add the fragrance of a flower.

II.

The breath of dawn
Proclaims thee coming, 'ere thou comest, dear:
About the shadowy lawn
Thy voice I hear.
The breeze of noon
With my fair locks shall fan thy brow, and I,
Thy lover, soon
With loving arms will form thy noontide canopy.

III.

My joy is full;
The bright sun gleams above the western flood,
And languid breezes lull
The dreaming wood.
Fair is my lot,
With fairy locks to shade thee; fair thy rest;
O love, wake not!
O bright sun, fail not, fail not in the golden west!

XARIFA. II.

"En el agua fria
Encendèis mi fuego."

I.

Fair galley, rest
In the golden west!
Lull him to sleep,
On the cold calm breast
Of the passionless deep;
Lull him, O lull him to sleep!

II.

Ah me, Ah me,
Would that I, with thee,
Might float at rest!
For the lone sad sea
Bears my love on its breast;
Lull him, O lull him to rest!

III.

Spread thy broad sail
To the morning gale;
Come to thy rest!
A breeze shall not fail
Thee, all day, from the west;
Lull him, O lull him to rest!

IV.

Fair galley, glide
On a tranquil tide
Home to thy rest!
The haven is wide,
And my sheltering breast
Yearns till it lull him to rest.

* * * *

V.

O sleep, love, sleep
Once more in the deep
Of my still breast!
While I weep, love, sleep,
In my fond arms prest,
Lull'd in my bosom to rest!

ZAGALA.

I.

'*Alma mia!* Since thy truest
Leaves thee, show him what thou doest.'
   'As my love doth, so I do,
   Love him truly, being true.'

II.

'Yet, before I pass away,
Dost thou share my sorrow, say?'
   'Silent grief can deftly tell
   All the sadness of Farewell.'

III.

'Stillness of my soul's unrest,
Speak the sadness of thy breast.'
   'If thy soul's unrest be still'd
   Then is all my wish fulfill'd.'

IV.

'When thy love hath left thee, say
How the slow hours wear away?'
  'Striving if I still may see,
  Where I saw thee, aught of thee?'

V.

'But, if eye and memory fail,
Will thy constant thought prevail?'
  'Folded art thou in my heart,
  Nearest ever when apart.'

VI.

'Yet convince me, dear, that thou,
Absent, wilt be true as now.'
  'Do I love thee, present? So,
  Absent, I shall fonder grow.'

VII.

'Wilt thou bind thy willing heart?
Seal the bond thus, ere we part.'
  'Love, thy kiss shall ever rest
  On my lips, thou in my breast.'

JUAN DE LINARES.

JUANA. I.

I.

I know not what this phantom is that wanders
  About the brain:
My lone heart knoweth not, but darkly ponders
  Upon its pain.

II.

I hear the sad sea moaning round the bases
  Of the lone hills:
Sad as the sea, sad memory embraces
  Wide tract of ills;

III.

Dim hopes which glimmer like to distant mountains
  In fading light,
Thro' tears which flow like never-failing fountains
  By day and night.

JUANA. II.

I.

ARE tears of any profit,
 By night or day?
When love hath past away
From sight, is aught left of it?
 Say, sister, say.

II.

Is love which passeth kinder
 Than grief which stays?
Thro' lone nights and long days
Sorrow hath naught to bind her,
 Yet sadly stays.

III.

Ah, tell me, sister, truly,
 Is sorrow kind?
Doth she not sadly bind,
That, coming, love may duly
 Due welcome find?

A SERENADE.

I.

In the sad starlight
  Vigil I keep;
By the glad starlight
  Sweet, my love, sleep!
Chill is the night, love,
  Sad without thee;
Hast thou in sleep, love,
  One sigh for me?

II.

Soft are thy lips, love,
  Sweet is thy breath;
Hard is thy heart, love,
  Bitter is death;
Yet sweet is bitter,
  Bitter is sweet;
Soft is death's litter
  Laid at thy feet.

III.

In the sad dawning
    Vigil I keep;
All the glad morning
    Sweet, my love, sleep!
Gather thy tresses
    Of gold* to thy breast;
Grey morning presses,
    I haste to my rest.

IV.

Fold thine arms close, love;
    Sadly I wend;
Sighing for thee, love,
    Unto my end;
Sighing for thee, love,
    All the sad night,
Dying for thee, love,
    In the grey light.

---

* *Las madejas de oro.*

ENGLISH LYRICS.

A FRAGMENT.

I.

Why not reminded be of hours so brief
 And glorious?
Dwells not a beauty in the Autumn leaf?
And over memory's lingering joy is grief
 Victorious?

II.

Is there no meaning in the having been
 Once bless'd?
Can winter leaves still hold a summer green?
Or think you ancient wrongs have never been
 Redress'd?

III.

Doth not joy linger in the silver cones
 Of mountains?
Which gleam in sunlight of the western zones
While o'er the plain night sweeps with all its moans
 Of fountains?

WATER-TONES.

I.

The still sad town oppresses me;
The Minster bell beats on my brain
Its monotone of ancient pain;
But here, the low sweet sobbing of the rivulet
blesses me.

II.

O brooklet, sob, and sigh, and fret;
Lone Miasótis dips her blue,
The bracken rusts with Autumn dew,
And all things droop and wear the tearful aspect
of regret.

III.

O brooklet, babble on in sorrow;
Garrulous was thy ripple of yore,
When young love stirr'd the heart's fresh core,
And young life wore from Spring to Summer.
Babble on in sorrow.

IV.

Tell out thy tale of hearts unblest,
Of hands that cling to faded flowers,
Or wrestle with the hopeless hours;
For in the deep eternal these and thou shalt
be at rest.

'ON REVIENT TOUJOURS.'

I.

Tears are dry, old vows are broken,
  Dost forget?
Were those mute vows never spoken,
  Eyes ne'er wet?

Clings the grey mist to the mountain
  As before?
Shrills the mavis by the fountain
  As of yore?

Doth the perfumed rose still charm thee,
  Or frail musk?
Night-dews were not wont to harm thee
  In the dusk.

Come and hear the rain-drop patter
  In the brook:
Come; faint moonbeams will not flatter
  Thy wan look.

Come; a faded flower shall greet thee
  Past its bloom:
Come; a once glad step shall meet thee
  In the gloom.

 * * * * *

Still the myriad chafer humming
  In deep shade:
Hark, I hear soft footsteps coming
  Down the glade.

Who is this that cometh sadly
  Down the glade?
Peace, fond heart, that boundest madly
  In deep shade!

Love, thy cheek and brow are pallid,
    Cold thy breath :
Would that vows once breathed were valid
    Unto death!

All thy vows they said were broken;
    Bitter jest!
Nearer, love; I see my token
    In thy breast.

Nearer, love; thine eyes are filling;
    Dost thou fear?
Simple faith strong doubt is killing
    With a tear.

Nearer to my breast she clingeth
    Than before :
Fairer tints the fair dawn bringeth
    Than of yore.

'ON REVIENT TOUJOURS.'

II.

I.

Hast thou forgotten
 Thine ancient vow?
Wilt thou recal it?
 Recal it now.
Others have told me,
 Come tell me thou,
Hast thou forgotten
 Thine ancient vow?

II.

Others have told me,
 Come, let me hear;
Put thy sweet lips, love,
 Close to mine ear;
Softly, not sadly,
 No, not a tear;
Grief cometh gladly
 If thou art near.

III.

Are thine arms round me
   Tenderly, now?
Hath a spell bound me,
   Or is it thou?
If it be thou, love,
   Come tell me now,
Hast thou forgotten
   Thine ancient vow?

MIRANDA. I.

"Forget-me-not."

I.

Fair flower, I seek thee, year by year,
    On land-lock'd pool or river;
    Where reed and bulrush glance and quiver
Thy voice I hear,
    'Forget-me-not.'

II.

O blossom still by lonely rill;
    And round my lady's bower,
    Uplift thy little voice, sweet flower,
And murmur still,
    'Forget-me-not.'

III.

O whisper to her in day dreams;
    And where she walks demurely
  Gaze up into her pure eyes purely,
By crystal streams,
    'Forget-me-not'!

IV.

O grow about her dainty feet
    By water-courses lonely,
  And murmur thou thy sweet name, only
Than hers less sweet,
    'Forget-me-not'!

MIRANDA. II.

> "But you——
> ——— are created
> Of every blossom's best."
>
> THE TEMPEST.

I.

No bud for thy bosom to-day, dear,
    No wreath for thy lily-brow;
The white Lily droops in the vale, dear,
    The red Rose fails on the bough;

II.

Her frail petals languish and droop, dear;
    Lost is the tint that I seek;
The crimson has past to thy lip, dear,
    The bloom to thy sunny cheek.

III.

The Columbine pales in the wood, dear,
    The frail Harebell on the wold;
Thine eyes pale not, and thy locks, dear,
    Like the trees, are strew'd with gold.

IV.

Sweet Summer has past with the bloom, dear,
    Of flower and blossom and tree,
Fair memory lightens the gloom, dear,
    With glimpses of those and of thee.

HOMEWARD-BOUND.

I.

So late: past hope: it cannot be:
So many weary years at sea,
The wanderer doubts if that can be—
That dim blue line—reality;
Or if the horizon mock his sight
With feint of land, at fading light
Of dying day, with hope too bright
To cheer him thro' the gloom of night,
And dawn upon the morrow still serene and bright.

II.

Past hope: tho' weary eyes may pale,
And heart must sink, before the veil
Of envious night, which yields too slowly
Her place to sunrise calm and holy;

At early dawn that purple line
Reveals a wished-for realm of pine
That climb steep cliffs which glance and shine
And lave their feet in sunlit brine:
So, love, a dawn past hope, your eyes reveal to
    mine.

THE END.

CAMBRIDGE: PRINTED BY JONATHAN PALMER.

186, Fleet Street,
December, 1863.

Messrs. BELL and DALDY'S
NEW AND STANDARD PUBLICATIONS.

New Books.

JERUSALEM Explored; being a Description of the Ancient and Modern City, with upwards of One Hundred Illustrations, consisting of Views, Ground-plans, and Sections. By Dr. Ermete Pierotti, Doctor of Mathematics, Architect-Engineer to His Excellency Soorraya Pasha of Jerusalem, and Architect of the Holy Land. (Translated by the Rev. T. G. Bonney, M.A., Fellow of St. John's College, Cambridge.) 2 vols. impl. 4to. 5*l.* 5*s.* [*Immediately.*

The Customs and Traditions of Palestine compared with the Bible, from Observations made during a Residence of Eight Years. By Dr. Ermete Pierotti. 8vo. [*Preparing.*

British Seaweeds. Drawn from Professor Harvey's "Phycologia Britannica," with Descriptions in popular language by Mrs. Alfred Gatty. 4to. 3*l.* 3*s.* [*Ready.*
This volume contains drawings of the British Seaweeds in 803 figures, with descriptions of each, including all the newly discovered species; an Introduction, an Amateur's Synopsis, Rules for preserving and laying out Seaweeds, and the Order of their arrangement in the Herbarium.

Host and Guest: a Book about Dinners, Wines, and Desserts. By A. V. Kirwan, of the Inner Temple, Esq. Crown 8vo. [*Shortly.*

Alexander Hamilton and his Contemporaries; or, the Founders of the American Republic. By C. J. Riethmuller, Esq., Author of "Teuton, a Poem," "Frederick Lucas," a Biography. [*In the press.*

The Decline of the Roman Republic. By George Long, M.A. 8vo. Vol. I. [*In the press.*

Isaiah's Testimony for Jesus. With an Historical Appendix, and Copious Tabular View of the Chronology, from the Original Authorities. By William Brown Galloway, M.A., Incumbent of St. Mark's, Regent's Park, and Chaplain to the Right Hon. Viscount Hawarden. 8vo. 14s. [*Ready.*

The Book of Psalms; a New Translation, with Introductions and Notes, Critical and Explanatory. By the Rev. J. J. Stewart Perowne, B.D., Fellow of C. C. College, Cambridge, and Examining Chaplain to the Lord Bishop of Norwich. 8vo. Vol. 1. [*Shortly.*

Life, Law, and Literature; Essays on Various Subjects. By William G. T. Barter, Esq., Barrister at Law. Fcap. 8vo. 5s. [*Ready.*

The Afternoon Lectures on English Literature. Delivered in the Theatre of the Museum of Industry, St. Stephen's Green, Dublin, in May and June, 1863. By the Rev. James Byrne, M.A., William Rushton, M.A., John K. Ingram, LL.D., Arthur Houston, M.A., the Rev. Edward Whately, M.A., Randal W. M'Donnell, Esq. Fcap. 8vo. 5s. [*Ready.*

The Divine Authority of the Pentateuch Vindicated. By Daniel Moore, M.A., Incumbent of Camden Church, Camberwell. Cr. 8vo. 6s. 6d. [*Ready.*

Bishop Colenso's Examination of the Pentateuch Examined. By the Rev. G. S. Drew, Author of "Scripture Lands," "Reasons of Faith." Crown 8vo. 3s. 6d. [*Ready.*

A Commentary on the Gospels for the Sundays and other Holy Days of the Christian Year. By the Rev. W. Denton, A.M., Worcester College, Oxford; and Incumbent of St. Bartholomew's, Cripplegate. 3 Vols. 8vo. 42s. [*Ready.*
Separately.
Vol. I. Advent to Easter. 15s.
Vol. II. Easter to the Sixteenth Sunday after Trinity. 14s.
Vol. III. Seventeenth Sunday after Trinity to Advent, and other Holy Days. 13s.

Daily Readings for a Year, on the Life of our Lord and Saviour Jesus Christ. By the Rev. Peter Young, M.A. *Third Edition, improved.* 2 vols. 8vo. 21s. Antique calf, 36s. Morocco, 40s. [*Ready.*

Notes and Dissertations, principally on Difficulties in the Scriptures of the New Covenant. By A. H. Wratislaw, M.A., Head Master of King Edward VI. Grammar School, Bury St. Edmunds, formerly Fellow and Tutor of Christ's College, Cambridge. 8vo. 7s. 6d. [*Ready.*

School Sermons. By the Rev. A. Jessopp, M.A., Head Master of the Grammar School, Norwich. Fcap. 8vo. [*In the press.*

The Book of Common Prayer. Ornamented with Head-pieces and Initial Letters specially designed for this edition. Printed in red and black at the Cambridge University Press. 24mo. Best morocco, 10s. 6d. Also in ornamental bindings, at various prices. [*Ready.*

Also a large paper Edition, crown 8vo. Best morocco, 18s. Also in ornamental bindings, at various prices. [*Ready.*

The Odes and Carmen Sæculare of Horace. Translated into English Verse by John Conington, M.A., Corpus Professor of Latin in the University of Oxford. *Second Edition.* Fcap. 8vo. Roxburgh binding, 5s. 6d.

On the Influence of Mechanical and Physiological Rest in the Treatment of Accidents and Surgical Diseases, and the Diagnostic Value of Pain. A course of Lectures, delivered at the Royal College of Surgeons of England in the years 1860, 1861, and 1862. By John Hilton, F.R.S., F.R.C.S., Member of the Council of the Royal College of Surgeons of England, late Professor of Anatomy and Surgery to the College, Surgeon and Lecturer on Surgery at the University of London, &c., &c. 8vo. 16s. [Ready.

A Fourth Series of Parables from Nature. By Mrs. Alfred Gatty. 16mo. 2s. [Immediately.

Baptista: A Quiet Story. With a Frontispiece. Crown 8vo. 6s. [Ready.

The Feasts of Camelot, with the Tales that were told there. By Mrs. T. K. Hervey. Fcap. 8vo. 4s. 6d. [Ready.

Arnold Delahaize; or, the Huguenot Pastor. With a Frontispiece. Fcap. 8vo. 5s. [Ready.

Denise. By the Author of "Mademoiselle Mori." 2 vols. Fcap. 8vo. 10s. [Ready.

The Adventures of a Little French Boy. With 50 Illustrations. Crown 8vo. Uniform with "Andersen's Tales," and "Robinson Crusoe." Cloth, gilt edges, 7s. 6d. [Ready.

Katie; or the Simple Heart. By D. Richmond, Author of "Annie Maitland." Illustrated by M. I. Booth. Crown 8vo. 6s. [Ready.

Glimpses into Petland. By the Rev. J. G. Wood, M. A., with Frontispiece by Crane. Fcap. 8vo. 3s. 6d. [Ready.

Mildred's Last Night; or, the Franklyns. By the Author of "Aggesden Vicarage." Fcap. 8vo. 4s. 6d. [Ready.

The Jew. A Poem. By Frederick Cerny. Fcap. 8vo. 2s. 6d. [Ready.

Poems and Songs, some of which are rendered from the Spanish. By Charles Welsh Mason. Fcap. 8vo. [Ready.

Original Acrostics. By a Circle of Friends. Fcap. 8vo. 2s. 6d. [Ready.

Dual Arithmetic. A New Art, by Oliver Byrne, formerly Professor of Mathematics at the late College of Civil Engineers, Putney. 8vo. 10s. 6d. [Ready.

Prosateurs Contemporains: or Selections in Prose, chiefly from contemporary French Literature. With English Notes. By F. E. A. Gasc. Fcap. 8vo. 5s. [Ready.

Chronological Maps. By D. Beale, author of "The Text-Book of English and General History."
No. I. England. 2s. 6d. [Ready.
No. II. Ancient History. 2s. [Ready.
Or bound together in One Vol., 3s. 6d.

**BELL and DALDY'S POCKET VOLUMES.** A Series of Select Works of Favourite Authors, adapted for general reading, moderate in price, compact and elegant in form, and executed in a style fitting them to be permanently preserved. Imperial 32mo.

Now Ready.

Burns's Poems. 2s. 6d.
Burns's Songs. 2s. 6d.
Walton's Complete Angler. Illustrated. 2s. 6d.
Sea Songs and Ballads. By Charles Dibdin and others. 2s. 6d.
White's Natural History of Selborne. 3s.
Coleridge's Poems. 2s. 6d.
The Robin Hood Ballads. 2s. 6d.
The Midshipman.—Autobiographical Sketches of his own early Career, by Capt. Basil Hall, R.N., F.R.S. From his " Fragments of Voyages and Travels." 3s.
The Lieutenant and Commander. By the same Author. 3s.
Southey's Life of Nelson. 2s. 6d.

Longfellow's Poems. 2s. 6d.
Lamb's Tales from Shakspeare. 2s.6d.
George Herbert's Poems. 2s.
George Herbert's Works. 3s.
Milton's Paradise Lost. 2s. 6d.
Milton's Paradise Regained and other Poems. 2s. 6d.

Preparing.

Walton's Lives of Donne, Wotton, Hooker, &c.
The Conquest of India. By Capt. Basil Hall, R.N.
Gray's Poems.
Goldsmith's Poems.
Goldsmith's Vicar of Wakefield.
Henry Vaughan's Poems.
And others.

In cloth, top edge gilt, at 6d. per volume extra; in half morocco, Roxburgh style, at 1s. extra; in antique or best plain morocco (Hayday) at 4s. extra.

**DR. RICHARDSON'S** New Dictionary of the English Language. Combining Explanation with Etymology, and copiously illustrated by Quotations from the best authorities. *New Edition*, with a Supplement containing additional Words and further Illustrations. In Two Vols. 4to. 4l. 14s. 6d. Half bound in russia, 5l. 15s. 6d. Russia, 6l. 12s.

The WORDS—with those of the same Family—are traced to their Origin.

The EXPLANATIONS are deduced from the Primitive Meaning through the various Usages.

The QUOTATIONS are arranged Chronologically, from the Earliest Period to the Present Time.

*** The Supplement separately, 4to. 12s.

Also, AN EDITION TO BE COMPLETED in 20 Monthly Parts. Price 4s. 6d. each. Parts 1 to 11 *now ready*.

AN 8VO. EDITION, without the Quotations, 15s. Half-russia, 20s. Russia, 24s.

"It is an admirable addition to our Lexicography, supplying a great desideratum, as exhibiting the biography of each word—its birth, parentage and education, the changes that have befallen it, the company it has kept, and the connexions it has formed—by rich series of quotations, all in chronological order. This is such a Dictionary as perhaps no other language could ever boast."—*Quarterly Review*.

Dr. Richardson on the Study of Language: an Exposition of Horne Tooke's Diversions of Purley. Fcap. 8vo. 4s. 6d.

The Library of English Worthies.

A Series of reprints of the best Authors carefully edited and collated with the Early Copies, and handsomely printed by Whittingham in Octavo.

SPENSER'S Complete Works; with Life, Notes, and Glossary, by John Payne Collier, Esq., F.S.A. 5 vols. 3*l*. 15*s*. Antique calf, 6*l*. 6*s*.

Herbert's Poems and Remains; with S. T. Coleridge's Notes, and Life by Izaak Walton. Revised, with additional Notes, by Mr. J. Yeowell. 2 vols. 1*l*. 1*s*. Morocco, antique calf or morocco, 2*l*. 2*s*.

Bishop Butler's Analogy of Religion; with Analytical Index, by the Rev. Edward Steere, LL.D. 12*s*. Antique calf, 1*l*. 1*s*.
"The present edition has been furnished with an Index of the Texts of Scripture quoted, and an Index of Words and Things considerably fuller than any hitherto published."—*Editor's Preface.*

Bishop Jeremy Taylor's Rule and Exercises of Holy Living and Dying. 2 vols. 1*l*. 1*s*. Morocco, antique calf or morocco, 2*l*. 2*s*.

Gower's Confessio Amantis, with Life by Dr. Pauli, and a Glossary. 3 vols. 2*l*. 2*s*. Antique calf, 3*l*. 6*s*. Only a limited number of Copies printed.
This important work is so scarce that it can seldom be met with even in large libraries. It is wanting in nearly every collection of English Poetry.

Uniform with the above.

The Physical Theory of Another Life. By Isaac Taylor, Esq. Author of "Logic in Theology," "Ultimate Civilization, &c." New Edition. 10*s*. 6*d*. Antique calf, 21*s*.

HISTORY of England, from the Invasion of Julius Cæsar to the end of the Reign of George II., by Hume and Smollett. With the Continuation, to the Accession of Queen Victoria, by the Rev. T. S. Hughes, B.D. late Canon of Peterborongh. *New Edition,* containing Historical Illustrations, Autographs, and Portraits, copious Notes, and the Author's last Corrections and Improvements. In 18 vols. crown 8vo. 4*s*. each.

Vols. I. to VI. (Hume's portion), 1*l*. 4*s*.
Vols. VII. to X. (Smollett's ditto), 16*s*.
Vols. XI. to XVIII. (Hughes's ditto), 1*l*. 12*s*.

History of England, from the Accession of George III. to the Accession of Queen Victoria. By the Rev. T. S. Hughes, B.D. *New Edition,* almost entirely re-written. In 7 vols. 8vo. 3*l*. 13*s*. 6*d*.

The Aldine Edition of the British Poets.

The Publishers have been induced, by the scarcity and increasing value of this admired Series of the Poets, to prepare a New Edition, very carefully corrected, and improved by such additions as recent literary research has placed within their reach.

The general principle of Editing which has been adopted is *to give the entire Poems of each author in strict conformity with the Edition which received his final revision, to prefix a Memoir, and to add such notes as may be necessary to elucidate the sense of obsolete words or explain obscure allusions.* Each author will be placed in the hands of a competent editor specially acquainted with the literature and bibliography of the period.

Externally this new edition will resemble the former, but with some improvements. It will be elegantly printed by Whittingham, on toned paper manufactured expressly for it; and a highly-finished portrait of each author will be given.

The *Aldine Edition of the British Poets* has hitherto been the favourite Series with the admirers of choice books, and every effort will be made to increase its claims as a comprehensive and faithful mirror of the poetic genius of the nation.

AKENSIDE'S Poetical Works, with Memoir by the Rev. A. Dyce, and additional Letters, carefully revised. 5s. Morocco, or antique morocco, 10s. 6d.

Collins's Poems, with Memoir and Notes by W. Moy Thomas, Esq. 3s. 6d. Morocco, or antique morocco, 8s. 6d.

Gray's Poetical Works, with Notes and Memoir by the Rev. John Mitford. 5s. Morocco, or antique morocco, 10s. 6d.

Kirke White's Poems, with Memoir by Sir H. Nicolas, and additional notes. Carefully revised. 5s. Morocco, or antique morocco, 10s. 6d.

Shakespeare's Poems, with Memoir by the Rev. A. Dyce. 5s. Morocco, or antique morocco, 10s. 6d.

Young's Poems, with Memoir by the Rev. John Mitford, and additional Poems. 2 vols. 10s. Morocco, or antique morocco, 1l. 1s.

Thomson's Poems, with Memoir by Sir H. Nicolas, annotated by Peter Cunningham, Esq., F.S.A., and additional Poems, carefully revised. 2 vols. 10s. Morocco, or antique morocco, 1l. 1s.

Thomson's Seasons, and Castle of Indolence, with Memoir. 6s. Morocco, or antique morocco, 11s. 6d.

Dryden's Poetical Works, with Memoir by the Rev. R. Hooper, F.S.A. Carefully revised. 5 vols. [*In the Press.*

Cowper's Poetical Works, including his Translations. Edited, with Memoir, by John Bruce, Esq., F.S.A. 3 vols. [*In the Press.*

Uniform with the Aldine Edition of the Poets.

The Works of Gray, edited by the Rev. John Mitford. With his Correspondence with Mr. Chute and others, Journal kept at Rome, Criticism on the Sculptures, &c. *New Edition.* 5 vols. 1*l*. 5*s*.

The Temple and other Poems. By George Herbert, with Coleridge's Notes. *New Edition.* 5*s*. Morocco, antique calf or morocco, 10*s*. 6*d*.

Vaughan's Sacred Poems and Pious Ejaculations, with Memoir by the Rev. H. F. Lyte. *New Edition.* 5*s*. Antique calf or morocco, 10*s*. 6*d*. Large Paper, 7*s*. 6*d*. Antique calf, 14*s*. Antique morocco, 15*s*.

"Preserving all the piety of George Herbert, they have less of his quaint and fantastic turns, with a much larger infusion of poetic feeling and expression."—*Lyte.*

Bishop Jeremy Taylor's Rule and Exercises of Holy Living and Holy Dying. 2 vols. 2*s*. 6*d*. each. Morocco, antique calf or morocco, 7*s*. 6*d*. each. In one volume, 5*s*. Morocco, antique calf or morocco, 10*s*. 6*d*.

Bishop Butler's Analogy of Religion; with Analytical Introduction and copious Index, by the Rev. Dr. Steere. 6*s*. Antique calf, 11*s*. 6*d*.

Bishop Butler's Sermons and Remains; with Memoir, by the Rev. E. Steere, LL.D. 6*s*.

*** This volume contains some additional remains, which are copyright, and render it the most complete edition extant.

Bishop Butler's Complete Works; with Memoir by the Rev. Dr. Steere. 2 vols. 12*s*.

Bacon's Advancement of Learning. Edited, with short Notes, by the Rev. G. W. Kitchin, M.A., Christ Church, Oxford. 6*s*.; antique calf, 11*s*. 6*d*.

Bacon's Essays; or, Counsels Civil and Moral, with the Wisdom of the Ancients. With References and Notes by S. W. Singer, F.S.A. 5*s*. Morocco, or antique calf, 10*s*. 6*d*.

Bacon's Novum Organum. Newly translated, with short Notes, by the Rev. Andrew Johnson, M.A. 6*s*. Antique calf, 11*s*. 6*d*.

Locke on the Conduct of the Human Understanding; edited by Bolton Corney, Esq., M. R. S. L. 3*s*. 6*d*. Antique calf, 8*s*. 6*d*.

"I cannot think any parent or instructor justified in neglecting to put this little treatise into the hands of a boy about the time when the reasoning faculties become developed."—*Hallam.*

Ultimate Civilization. By Isaac Taylor, Esq. 6*s*.

Logic in Theology, and other Essays. By Isaac Taylor, Esq. 6*s*.

The Thoughts of the Emperor M. Aurelius Antoninus. Translated by George Long. 6*s*.

The Schole Master. By Roger Ascham. Edited, with copious Notes and a Glossary, by the Rev. J. E. B. Mayor, M.A. 6*s*.

Domestic Life in Palestine. By M. E. Rogers. Second Edition. Post 8vo. 10s. 6d.

Servia and the Servians. By the Rev. W. Denton, M.A. With Illustrations. Crown 8vo. 9s. 6d.

By-Roads and Battle Fields in Picardy: with Incidents and Gatherings by the Way between Ambleteuse and Ham; including Agincourt and Crécy. By G. M. Musgrave, M.A., Illustrated. Super-royal 8vo. 16s.

The Boat and the Caravan. A Family Tour through Egypt and Syria. New and cheaper Edition. Fcap. 8vo. 5s. 6d.

Fragments of Voyages and Travels. By Captain Basil Hall, R.N. 1st, 2nd, and 3rd Series in 1 vol. complete. Royal 8vo. 10s. 6d.

An Old Man's Thoughts about Many Things. Being Essays on Schools, Riches, Statues, Books, Place and Power, The Final Cause, &c. Crown 8vo. 7s. 6d.

Frederick Lucas. A Biography. By C. J. Riethmüller, author of "Teuton," a Poem. Crown 8vo. 4s. 6d.

Adventures of Baron Wenceslas Wratislaw of Mitrowitz; what he saw in the Turkish Metropolis, Constantinople, experienced in his Captivity, and, after his happy return to his country, committed to writing, in the year of our Lord, 1599. Literally translated from the original Bohemian by A. H. Wratislaw, M.A. Crown 8vo. 6s. 6d.

Legends of the Lintel and the Ley. By Walter Cooper Dendy. Crown 8vo. 9s.

The Gem of Thorney Island; or, The Historical Associations of Westminster Abbey. By the Rev. J. Ridgway, M.A. Crown 8vo. 7s. 6d.

Gifts and Graces. A new Tale, by the Author of "The Rose and the Lotus." Post 8vo. 7s. 6d.

Childhood and Youth. By Count Nicola Tolstoi. Translated from the Russian by Malwida von Meysenbug. Post 8vo. 8s. 6d.

Baronscliffe; or, the Deed of other Days. By Mrs. P. M. Latham, Author of "The Wayfarers." Crown 8vo. 6s.

The Manse of Mastland. Sketches: Serious and Humorous, in the Life of a Village Pastor in the Netherlands. Translated from the Dutch by Thomas Keightley, M.A. Post 8vo. 9s.

The Leadbeater Papers: a Selection from the MSS. and Correspondence of Mary Leadbeater, containing her Annals of Ballitore, with a Memoir of the Author; Unpublished Letters of Edmund Burke; and the Correspondence of Mrs. R. Trench and Rev. G. Crabbe. Second Edition. 2 vols. crown 8vo. 14s.

The Home Life of English Ladies in the Seventeenth Century. By the Author of "Magdalen Stafford." Second Edition, enlarged. Fcap. 8vo. 6s. Calf, 9s. 6d.

The Romance and its Hero. By the Author of "Magdalen Stafford." 2 vols. Fcap. 8vo. 12s.

Magdalen Stafford. A Tale. Fcap. 8vo. 5s.

Mrs. Alfred Gatty's Popular Works.

"Mrs. Gatty is *facile princeps* in the art of writing for the young. She is to the altered tastes of this generation almost what Miss Edgeworth was to the last. And we have the rare satisfaction of knowing that Mrs. Gatty's usefulness will not terminate with herself. Her peculiar talent is hereditary. 'Melchior's Dream' is the production of the veritable 'Aunt Judy' herself, and the very pretty illustrations which adorn it are from the pencil of another sister."—*Guardian.*

PARABLES from Nature; with Notes on the Natural History. Illustrated by W. Holman Hunt, Otto Speckter, C. W. Cope, R. A., E. Warren, W. Millais, G. Thomas, and H. Calderon. 8vo. Ornamental cloth, 10s. 6d. Antique morocco elegant, 1l. 1s.

Parables from Nature. 16mo. with Illustrations. First Series. *Eleventh Edition.* 1s. 6d. Second Series. *Sixth Edition.* 2s. Or the two Series in one volume. 3s. 6d. Third Series (Red Snow and other Parables). *Second Edition.* 2s. Fourth Series. [*In the press.*

Worlds not Realized. 16mo. *Third Edition.* 2s.

Proverbs Illustrated. 16mo. with Illustrations. *3rd Edition.* 2s.

⁎ These little works have been found useful for Sunday reading in the family circle, and instructive and interesting to school children.

Aunt Judy's Tales. Illustrated by Clara S. Lane. Fcap. 8vo. *Fourth Edition.* 3s. 6d.

Aunt Judy's Letters. Illustrated by Clara S. Lane. Fcap. 8vo. 3s. 6d.

The Human Face Divine, and other Tales. With Illustrations by C. S. Lane. Fcap. 8vo. 3s. 6d.

The Fairy Godmothers and other Tales. *Fourth Edition.* Fcap. 8vo. with Frontispiece. 2s. 6d.

Legendary Tales. With Illustrations by Phiz. Fcap. 8vo. 5s.

The Poor Incumbent. Fcap. 8vo. Sewed, 1s. Cloth, 1s. 6d.

The Old Folks from Home; or, a Holiday in Ireland. *Second Edition.* Post 8vo. 7s. 6d.

Melchior's Dream, and other Tales. By J. H. G. Edited by Mrs. Gatty. Illustrated. Fcap. 8vo. 3s. 6d.

By the late Mrs. Woodrooffe.

COTTAGE Dialogues. *New Edition.* 12mo. 4s. 6d.

Michael Kemp, the Happy Farmer's Lad. *8th Edition.* 12mo. 4s.

A Sequel to Michael Kemp. *New Edition.* 12mo. 6s. 6d.

THE Adventures of a Little French Boy. With 50 Illustrations. Crown 8vo. Cloth, gilt edges. 7s. 6d.

The Life and Adventures of Robinson Crusoe. By Daniel Defoe. With 100 Illustrations by E. H. Wehnert. Uniform with the above. Crown 8vo. Cloth, gilt edges. 7s. 6d.

Andersen's Tales for Children. Translated by A. Wehnert. With 105 Illustrations by E. H. Wehnert, W. Thomas, and others. Uniform with the above. Crown 8vo. Cloth, gilt edges. 7s. 6d.

Among the Tartar Tents; or, the Lost Fathers. A Tale By Anne Bowman, Author of " Esperanza," " The Boy Voyagers," &c. With Illustrations. Crown 8vo. 5s.

Little Maggie and her Brother. By Mrs. G. Hooper, Author of " Recollections of Mrs. Anderson's School," " Arbell," &c. With a Frontispiece. Fcap. 8vo. 2s. 6d.

Church Stories. Edited by the Rev. J. E. Clarke. Crown 8vo. 2s. 6d.

Cavaliers and Round Heads. By J. G. Edgar, Author of " Sea Kings and Naval Heroes." Illustrated by Amy Butts. Fcap. 8vo. 5s.

Sea-Kings and Naval Heroes. A Book for Boys. By J. G. Edgar. With Illustrations by C. K. Johnson and C. Keene. Fcap. 8vo. 5s.

The White Lady and Undine, translated from the German by the Hon. C. L. Lyttelton. With numerous Illustrations. Fcap. 8vo. 5s. Or, separately. 2s. 6d. each.

The Lights of the Will o' the Wisp. Translated by Lady Maxwell Wallace. With a coloured Frontispiece. Imperial 16mo. Cloth, gilt edges, 5s.

The Life of Christopher Columbus, in Short Words. By Sarah Crompton. Super royal 16mo. 2s. 6d. Also an Edition for Schools, 1s.

The Life of Martin Luther, in Short Words. By the same Author. Super royal 16mo. 1s. 6d. Stiff cover, 1s.

Guessing Stories; or, the Surprising Adventures of the Man with the Extra Pair of Eyes. A Book for Young People. By the Rev. Philip Freeman. Imperial 16mo. Cloth, gilt edges, 3s.

Redfield; or, a Visit to the Country. A Story for Children. With Four Illustrations by John Absolon. Super royal 16mo. 2s. 6d. Coloured, 3s. 6d.

Giles Witherne; or, The Reward of Disobedience. A Village Tale for the Young. By the Rev. J. P. Parkinson, D.C.L. Sixth Edition. Illustrated by the Rev. F. W. Mann. Super-royal 16mo. 1s. Cloth, gilt edges, 2s. 6d.

The Disorderly Family; or, the Village of R * * * *. A Tale for Young Persons. In Two Parts. By a Father. 6d.; Cloth, gilt edges, 1s.

Nursery Tales. By Mrs. Motherly. With Illustrations by C. S. Lane. Imperial 16mo. 2s. 6d. Coloured, gilt edges, 3s. 6d.

Nursery Poetry. By Mrs. Motherly. With Eight Illustrations by C. S. Lane. Imperial 16mo. 2s. 6d. Coloured, gilt edges, 3s. 6d.

A Poetry Book for Children. Illustrated with Thirty-seven highly-finished Engravings, by C. W. Cope, R. A., Helmsley. Palmer, Skill, Thomas, and H. Weir. *New Edition.* Crown 8vo. 2s. 6d.

Nursery Carols. Illustrated with 120 Pictures. By Ludwig Riether and Oscar Pletsch. Imperial 16mo. Ornamental Binding. 3s. 6d. Coloured, 6s.

Poetry for Play-Hours. By Gerda Fay. With Eight large Illustrations. Imperial 16mo. 3s. 6d. Coloured, gilt edges, 4s. 6d.

Very Little Tales for Very Little Children In single Syllables of *Four* and *Five* letters. *New Edition.* Illustrated. 2 vols. 16mo. 1s. 6d. each, or in 1 vol. 3s.

Progressive Tales for Little Children. In words of *One* and *Two* Syllables. Forming the sequel to " Very Little Tales." *New Edition.* Illustrated. 2 vols. 16mo. 1s. 6d. each, or in 1 vol. 3s.

Karl and the Six Little Dwarfs. By Julia Goddard. Illustrated. 16mo. 2s. 6d.

Charades, Enigmas, and Riddles. Collected by a Cantab. *Fourth Edition, enlarged.* Illustrated. Fcap. 8vo. 2s. 6d.

The Children's Picture Book Series.

Written expressly for Young People, super-royal 16mo.

Cloth, gilt edges, price 5s. each.

BIBLE Picture Book. Eighty Illustrations. (Coloured, 9s.)

Scripture Parables and Bible Miracles. Thirty-two Illustrations. (Coloured, 7s. 6d.)

English History. Sixty Illustrations. (Coloured, 9s.)

Good and Great Men. Fifty Illustrations. (Coloured, 9s.)

Useful Knowledge. One Hundred and Thirty Figures.

Cloth, red edges, price 2s. 6d. each. (*Coloured, gilt edges,* 3s. 6d.)

Scripture Parables. By Rev. J. E. Clarke. 16 Illustrations.

Bible Miracles. By Rev. J. E. Clarke, M.A. 16 Illustrations.

The Life of Joseph. Sixteen Illustrations.

Bunyan's Pilgrim's Progress. Sixteen Illustrations.

CLARK'S Introduction to Heraldry.—Containing Rules for Blazoning and Marshalling Coats of Armour—Dictionary of Terms—Orders of Knighthood explained—Degrees of the Nobility and Gentry—Tables of Precedency; 43 Engravings, including upwards of 1,000 Examples, and the Arms of numerous Families. *Sixteenth Edition improved*. Small 8vo. 7s. 6d. Coloured, 18s.

Book of Family Crests and Mottoes, with *Four Thousand Engravings* of the Crests of the Peers, Baronets, and Gentry of England and Wales, and Scotland and Ireland. A Dictionary of Mottos, &c. *Tenth Edition, enlarged*. 2 vols. small 8vo. 1l. 4s.

" Perhaps the best recommendation to its utility and correctness (in the main) is, that it has been used as a work of reference in the Heralds College. No wonder it sells."—*Spectator.*

The Architectural History of Chichester Cathedral, with an Introductory Essay on the Fall of the Tower and Spire. By the Rev. R. Willis, M.A., F.R.S., &c.—Of Boxgrove Priory, by the Rev. J. L. Petit, M.A., F.S.A.—And of Shoreham Collegiate Church, together with the Collective Architectural History of the foregoing buildings, as indicated by their mouldings, by Edmund Sharpe, M.A., F.R.I B.A. Illustrated by one hundred Plates, Diagrams, Plans and Woodcuts. Super-royal 4to. 1l. 10s.

Architectural Studies in France. By the Rev. J. L. Petit, M.A., F.S.A. With Illustrations from Drawings by the Author and P. H. Delamotte. Imp. 8vo. 2l. 2s.

Remarks on Church Architecture. With Illustrations. By the Rev. J. L. Petit, M.A. 2 vols. 8vo. 1l. 1s.

A Few Notes on the Temple Organ. By Edmund Macrory, M.A. *Second Edition*. Super-royal 16mo. Half morocco, Roxburgh, 3s. 6d.

Scudamore Organs, or Practical Hints respecting Organs for Village Churches and small Chancels, on improved principles. By the Rev. John Baron, M.A., Rector of Upton Scudamore, Wilts. With Designs by G. E. Street, F.S.A. *Second Edition, revised and enlarged*. 8vo. 6s.

The Bell; its Origin, History, and Uses. By Rev. A. Gatty. 3s.

Practical Remarks on Belfries and Ringers. By the Rev. H. T. Ellacombe, M.A., F.A.S., Rector of Clyst St. George, Devonshire. *Second Edition*, with an Appendix on Chiming. Illustrated. 8vo. 3s.

Engravings of Unedited or Rare Greek Coins. With Descriptions. By General C. R. Fox. 4to. Part I, Europe. Part II, Asia and Africa. 7s. 6d. each.

Proceedings of the Archæological Institute at Newcastle, in 1853. With Numerous Engravings. 2 vols. 8vo. 2l. 2s.

A Handbook for Visitors to Cambridge. By Norris Deck. With 8 Steel Engravings, 97 Woodcuts, and a Map. Crown 8vo. 5s.

Canterbury in the Olden Time: from the Municipal Archives and other Sources. By John Brent, F.S.A. With Illustrations. 5s.

Whirlwinds and Dust-Storms of India. By P. F. H. Baddeley. Large 8vo. With Illustrations, 8s. 6d.; without Illustrations, 3s.

Two Transparent Wind Cards in Horn, adapted to the Northern and Southern Hemispheres, for the use of Sailors. 2s.

New and Standard Publications. 13

EBSTER'S Complete Dictionary of the English Language. *New Edition*, revised and greatly enlarged, by CHAUNCEY A. GOODRICH, Professor in Yale College. 4to. (1624 pp.) 1*l*. 11*s*. 6*d*.; half calf, 2*l*.; calf, or half russia, 2*l*. 2*s*.; russia, 2*l*. 10*s*.

Though the circulation of Dr. Webster's celebrated Dictionary, in its various forms, in the United States, in England, and in every country where the English Language is spoken, may be counted by hundreds of thousands, it is believed that there are many persons to whom the book is yet unknown, and who, if seeking for a Dictionary which should supply all reasonable wants, would be at a loss to select one from the numerous competitors in the field.

In announcing this New Edition, the Proprietors desire to call attention to the features which distinguish it, and to put before those who are in want of such a book, the points in which it excels all other Dictionaries, and which render it the best that has as yet been issued for the practical purposes of daily use:—

1. Accuracy of Definition. 2. Pronunciation intelligibly marked. 3. Completeness. 4. Etymology. 5. Obsolete Words. 6. Uniformity in the Mode of Spelling. 7. Quotations. 8. Cheapness.

With the determination that the superiority of the work shall be fully maintained, and that it shall keep pace with the requirements of the age and the universal increase of education, the Proprietors have added to this New Edition, under the editorship of Professor Goodrich,—

A Table of Synonyms. An Appendix of New Words. Table of Quotations, Words, Phrases, &c.

Tables of Interest, enlarged and Improved; calculated at Five per Cent.; Showing at one view the Interest of any Sum, from £1 to £365: they are also carried on by hundreds to £1,000, and by thousands to £10,000, from one day to 365 days. To which are added, Tables of Interest, from one to 12 months, and from two to 13 years. Also Tables for calculating Commission on Sales of Goods or Banking Accounts, from ¼ to 5 per Cent., with several useful additions, among which are Tables for calculating Interest on large sums for 1 day, at the several rates of 4 and 5 per Cent. to £100,000,000. By Joseph King, of Liverpool. 24*th Edition*. With a Table showing the number of days from any one day to any other day in the Year. 8vo. 1*l*. 1*s*.

The Housekeeping Book, or Family Ledger. An Improved Principle, by which an exact Account can be kept of Income and Expenditure; suitable for any Year, and may be begun at any time. With Hints on Household Management, Receipts, &c. By Mrs. Hamilton. 8vo. Cloth, 1*s*. 6*d* sewed, 1*s*.

The Executor's Account Book, with short Practical Instructions for the guidance of Executors. By a Solicitor. Folio. 4*s*.

IGHTINGALE Valley; a Collection of Choice Lyrics and Short Poems. From the time of Shakespeare to the present day. Edited by William Allingham. Fcap. 8vo. 5*s*.; mor., antique calf or mor., 10*s*. 6*d*.

Legends and Lyrics, by Adelaide Anne Procter. *Seventh Edition*. Fcap. 5*s*. Antique or best plain morocco, 10*s*. 6*d*.

———— *Second Series. Third Edition.* Fcap. 8vo. 5*s*.; antique or best plain morocco, 10*s*. 6*d*.

Latin Translations of English Hymns. By Charles Buchanan Pearson, M.A., Rector of Knebworth. Fcap. 8vo. 5*s*.

Verses for Holy Seasons. By C. F. Alexander. Edited by the Very Rev. W. F. Hook, D.D. *4th Edition.* Fcap. 3s. 6d.; morocco, antique calf or morocco, 8s. 6d.

The Legend of the Golden Prayers, and other Poems. By the Same Author. Fcap. 8vo. 5s.; antique or best plain morocco, 10s. 6d.

Ballads and Songs. By Bessie Rayner Parkes. Fcap. 5s

The Story of Queen Isabel, and other Verses. By M. S. Fcap. 8vo. 3s. 6d.

Love and Mammon, and other Poems. By. F. S. Wyvill, Author of "Pansies." Fcap. 8vo. 5s.

The Frithiof Saga. A Poem. Translated from the Norwegian. By the Rev. R. Mucklestone, M.A., Rector of Dinedor. Cr. 8vo. 7s. 6d.

Saul, a Dramatic Poem; Elizabeth, an Historical Ode; and other Poems. By William Fulford, M.A. Fcap. 8vo. 5s.

Lays and Poems on Italy. By F. A. Mackay. Fcap. 8vo. 5s.

Poems from the German. By Richard Garnett, Author of "Io in Egypt, and other Poems." Fcap. 8vo. 3s. 6d.

Io in Egypt, and other Poems. By R. Garnett. Fcap. 8vo. 5s.

The Monks of Kilcrea, and other Poems. *3rd Edition.* Post. 7s. 6d.

Teuton. A Poem. By C. J. Riethmüller. Crown 8vo. 7s. 6d.

Dryope, and other Poems. By T. Ashe. Fcap. 8vo. 6s.

Wild Thyme. By E. M. Mitchell. Fcap. 8vo. 5s.

Lyrics and Idylls. By Gerda Fay. Fcap. 8vo. 4s.

David Mallet's Poems. With Notes and Illustrations by F. Dinsdale, LL.D., F.S.A. *New Edition.* Post 8vo. 10s. 6d.

Ballads and Songs of Yorkshire. Transcribed from private MSS., rare Broadsides, and scarce Publications; with Notes and a Glossary. By C. J. D. Ingledew, M.A., Ph.D., F.G.H.S., author of "The History of North Allerton." Fcap. 8vo. 6s.

Percy's Reliques of Ancient English Poetry. 3 vols. sm. 8vo. 15s. Half-bound, 18s. Antique calf, or morocco, 1l. 11s. 6d.

The Book of Ancient Ballad Poetry of Great Britain, Historical, Traditional and Romantic: with Modern Imitations, Translations, Notes and Glossary, &c. *New and Improved Edition.* 8vo. Half-bound, 14s. Antique morocco, 21s.

The Promises of Jesus Christ. Illuminated by Albert H. Warren, *Second Edition.* Ornamental cloth, 15s. Antique morocco elegant, 21s.

Christmas with the Poets: a Collection of English Poetry relating to the Festival of Christmas. Illustrated by Birket Foster, and with numerous initial letters and borders beautifully printed in gold and colours by Edmund Evans. *New and improved Edition.* Super royal 8vo. Ornamental binding, 21s. Antique morocco, 31s. 6d.

New and Standard Publications.

ATHENÆ Cantabrigienses. By C. H. Cooper, F.S.A., and Thompson Cooper. Volume I. 1500—1585. 8vo. 18s. Vol. II. 1586—1609. 8vo. 18s.

    This work, in illustration of the biography of notable and eminent men who have been members of the University of Cambridge, comprehends notices of:—1. Authors. 2. Cardinals, archbishops, bishops, abbots, heads of religious houses and other church dignitaries. 3. Statesmen, diplomatists, military and naval commanders. 4. Judges and eminent practitioners of the civil or common law. 5. Sufferers for religious or political opinions. 6. Persons distinguished for success in tuition. 7. Eminent physicians and medical practitioners. 8. Artists, musicians, and heralds. 9. Heads of colleges, professors, and principal officers of the university. 10. Benefactors to the university and colleges, or to the public at large.

The Early and Middle Ages of England. By C. H. Pearson, M.A., Fellow of Oriel College, Oxford, and Professor of Modern History, King's College, London. 8vo. 12s.

Choice Notes from "Notes and Queries," by the Editor. Fcap. 8vo. 5s. each.
    Vol. I.—History.   Vol. II.—Folk Lore.

Master Wace's Chronicle of the Conquest of England. Translated from the Norman by Sir Alexander Malet, Bart., H.B.M. Plenipotentiary, Frankfort. With Photograph Illustrations of the Bayeaux Tapestry. Medium 4to. Half-morocco, Roxburgh, 2l. 2s.

The Prince Consort's Addresses on Different Public Occasions. Beautifully printed by Whittingham. 4to. 10s. 6d.

Life and Books; or, Records of Thought and Reading. By J. F. Boyes, M.A. Fcap. 8vo. 5s.; calf, 8s. 6d.

Life's Problems. By Sir Rutherford Alcock, K.C.B. *Second Edition*, revised and enlarged. Fcap. 5s.

Parliamentary Short-Hand (Official System). By Thompson Cooper. Fcap. 8vo. 2s. 6d.
    This is the system *universally practised by the Government Official Reporters*. It has many advantages over the system ordinarily adopted, and has hitherto been inaccessible, except in a high-priced volume.

English Retraced; or, Remarks, Critical and Philological, founded on a Comparison of the Breeches Bible with the English of the present day. Crown 8vo. 5s.

The Pleasures of Literature. By R. Aris Willmott, M.A. *Fifth Edition*, enlarged. Fcap. 8vo. 5s. Morocco, 10s. 6d.

Hints and Helps for Youths leaving School. By the Rev. J. S. Gilderdale, M.A. Fcap. 8vo. 5s. Calf, 8s. 6d.

Hints for Pedestrians, Practical and Medical. By G. C. Watson, M.D. *Third Edition*, enlarged. Fcap. 8vo. 2s. 6d.

Hints to Maid Servants in Small Households, on Manners, Dress, and Duties. By Mrs. Motherly. Fcap. 8vo. 1s. 6d.

A Wife's Home Duties; containing Hints to inexperienced Housekeepers. Fcap. 8vo. 2s. 6d.

Geology in the Garden: or, The Fossils in the Flint Pebbles. With 106 Illustrations. By the Rev. Henry Eley, M.A. Fcap. 8vo. 6s.

British Beetles. Transferred in 259 plates from Curtis's " British Entomology;" with Descriptions by E. W. Janson, Esq., Secretary of the Entomological Society. 4to. 18s. Coloured, 1l. 11s. 6d. [Ready.

Halcyon: or Rod-Fishing with Fly, Minnow, and Worm. To which is added a short and easy method of dressing Flies, with a description of the materials used. By Henry Wade, Honorary Secretary to the Wear Valley Angling Association. With 8 Coloured Plates, containing 117 Specimens of natural and artificial Flies, Materials, &c., and 4 Plates illustrating Fishes, Baiting, &c. Cr. 8vo. 7s. 6d.

A Handy Book of the Chemistry of Soils: Explanatory of their Composition, and the Influence of Manures in ameliorating them, with Outlines of the various Processes of Agricultural Analysis. By John Scoffern, M.B. Crown 8vo. 4s. 6d.

Flax and its Products in Ireland. By William Charley, J. P., Juror and Reporter Class XIV, Great Exhibition 1851; also appointed in 1862 for Class XIX. With a Frontispiece. Crown 8vo. 5s.

The Odes and Carmen Sæculare of Horace. Translated into English Verse by John Conington, M.A., Corpus Professor of Latin in the University of Oxford. *Second Edition.* Fcap. 8vo. Roxburgh binding. 5s. 6d.

SERMONS.

ARISH SERMONS. By the Rev. M. F. Sadler, M.A., Vicar of Bridgwater. Author of " The Second Adam and the New Birth." Fcap. 8vo. Vol. I, Advent to Trinity; Vol. II, Trinity to Advent. 7s. 6d. each.

Twenty-four Sermons on Christian Doctrine and Practice, and on the Church, By C. J. Blomfield, D.D., late Lord Bishop of London. (*Hitherto unpublished.*) 8vo. 10s. 6d.

King's College Sermons. By the Rev. E. H. Plumptre, M.A., Divinity Professor. Fcap. 8vo. 2s. 6d.

Sermons preached in Westminster. By the Rev. C. F. Secretan, M.A., Incumbent of Holy Trinity, Vauxhall-Bridge Road. Fcap. 8vo. 6s.

Sermons. By the Rev. A. Gatty, D.D., Vicar of Ecclesfield. 12mo. 8s.

Twenty Plain Sermons for Country Congregations and Family Reading. By the Rev. A. Gatty, D.D., Vicar of Ecclesfield. Fcap. 5s.

Sermons to a Country Congregation—Advent to Trinity. By the Rev. Hastings Gordon, M.A. 12mo. 6s.

Sermons Suggested by the Miracles of our Lord and Saviour Jesus Christ. By the Very Rev. Dean Hook. 2 vols. Fcap. 8vo. 12s.

Five Sermons Preached before the University of Oxford. By the Very Rev. W. F. Hook, D.D., Dean of Chichester. *Third Edition.* 3s.

The Last Days of our Lord's Ministry : a Course of Lectures on the principal events of Passion Week. By Walter Farquhar Hook, D.D., F.R.S., Dean of Chichester. *New Edition.* Fcap. 8vo. 3s. 6d.

Sermons, chiefly Practical. By the Rev. T. Nunns, M A. Edited by the Very Rev. W. F. Hook, D.D., Dean of Chichester. Fcap. 8vo. 6s.

Sermons on Popular Subjects, preached in the Collegiate Church, Wolverhampton. By the Rev. Julius Lloyd, M. A. 8vo. 4s. 6d.

The Prodigal Son. Sermons by W. R. Clark, M.A., Vicar of Taunton, S. Mary Magdalene. Fcap. 8vo. 2s. 6d.

The Redeemer : a Series of Sermons on Certain Aspects of the Person and Work of our Lord Jesus Christ. By W. R. Clark, M.A., Vicar of Taunton. Fcap. 8vo. 5s.

The Fulness of the Manifestation of Jesus Christ ; being a Course of Epiphany Lectures. By Hilkiah Bedford Hall, B.C.L., Afternoon Lecturer of the Parish Church, Halifax, Author of " A Companion to the Authorized Version of the New Testament. Fcap. 8vo. 2s.

Parochial Sermons. By the Rev. D. G. Stacy, Vicar of Hornchurch, Essex. Fcap. 8vo. 5s.

Plain Parochial Sermons. By the Rev. C. F. C. Pigott, B.A., late Curate of St. Michael's, Handsworth. Fcap. 8vo. 6s.

Our Privileges, Responsibilities, and Trials. By the Rev. E. Phillips, M.A. Fcap. 8vo. 5s.

Sermons, Preached in the Parish Church of Godalming, Surrey, by the Rev. E. J. Boyce, M.A., Vicar. *Second Edition.* Fcap. 8vo. 6s.

Life in Christ. By the Rev. J. Llewellyn Davies, M.A., Rector of Christ Church, Marylebone. Fcap. 8vo. 5s.

The Church of England; its Constitution, Mission, and Trials. By the Rt. Rev. Bishop Broughton. Edited, with a Prefatory Memoir, by the Ven. Archdeacon Harrison. 8vo. 10s. 6d.

Plain Sermons, Addressed to a Country Congregation. By the late E. Blencowe, M.A. 1st and 3rd Series, fcap. 8vo. 7s. 6d. each.

Missionary Sermons preached at Hagley. Fcap. 3s. 6d.

The Sufficiency of Christ. Sermons preached during the Reading Lenten Mission of 1860. Fcap. 8vo. 2s. 6d.

Westminster Abbey Sermons for the Working Classes. Fcap. *Authorized Edition.* 1858. 2s.: 1859. 2s. 6d.

Sermons preached at St. Paul's Cathedral. *Authorized Edition.* 1859. Fcap. 8vo. 2s. 6d.

AILY Readings for a Year, on the Life of Our Lord and Saviour Jesus Christ. By the Rev. Peter Young, M.A. *Third Edition*, improved. 2 vols. 8vo. 1*l.* 1*s.* Antique calf, 1*l.* 16*s.* Morocco, Hayday, 2*l.*

Short Sunday Evening Readings, Selected and Abridged from various Authors by the Dowager Countess of Cawdor. In large type. 8vo. 5*s.*

A Commentary on the Gospels for the Sundays and other Holy Days of the Christian Year. By the Rev. W. Denton, A.M., Worcester College, Oxford, and Incumbent of St. Bartholomew's, Cripplegate. 3 vols. 8vo. 42*s.* Vol. 1. Advent to Easter, 15*s.* Vol. II. Easter to the Sixteenth Sunday after Trinity, 14*s.* Vol. III. Seventeenth Sunday after Trinity to Advent, and other Holy Days, 13*s.*

A Commentary, Critical, Exegetical, and Doctrinal, on St. Paul's Epistle to the Galatians: with a revised Translation. By George John Gwynne, A.B., Ex-Schol. T.C.D., Rector and Vicar of Wallstown, Diocese of Cloyne. 8vo. 12*s.*

The Second Adam, and the New Birth; or, the Doctrine of Baptism as contained in Holy Scripture. By the Rev. M. F. Sadler, M.A. Vicar of Bridgewater, Author of " The Sacrament of Responsibility." *Third Edition*, greatly enlarged. Fcap. 8vo. 4*s.* 6*d.*

The Sacrament of Responsibility; or, Testimony of the Scripture to the teaching of the Church on Holy Baptism, with especial reference to the Cases of Infants, and Answers to Objections. *Sixth Edition.* 6*d.*

Popular Illustrations of some Remarkable Events recorded in the Old Testament. By the Rev. J. F. Dawson, LL.B., Rector of Toynton. Post 8vo. 8*s.* 6*d.*

The Acts and Writings of the Apostles. By C. Pickering Clarke, M.A. Post 8vo. Vol. 1., with Map., 7*s.* 6*d.*

A Manual for Communion Classes and Communicant Meetings. Addressed specially to the Parish Priests and Deacons of the Church of England. By C. Pickering Clarke, M.A. Fcap. 8vo. 3*s.* 6*d.*

Memoir of a French New Testament, in which the Mass and Purgatory are found in the Sacred Text; together with Bishop Kidder's " Reflections " on the same. By Henry Cotton, D.C.L., Archdeacon of Cashel. *Second Edition, enlarged.* 8vo. 3*s.* 6*d.*

The Spirit of the Hebrew Poetry. By Isaac Taylor, Esq., Author of " The Natural History of Enthusiasm," " Ultimate Civilization," &c. 8vo. 10*s.* 6*d.*

The Wisdom of the Son of David: an Exposition of the First Nine Chapters of the Book of Proverbs. Fcap. 8vo. 5*s.*

A Companion to the Authorized Version of the New Testament: being Explanatory Notes, together with Explanatory Observations and an Introduction. By the Rev. H. B. Hall, B.C.L. *Second and cheaper Edition*, revised and enlarged. Fcap. 8vo. 3*s.* 6*d.*

Readings on the Morning and Evening Prayer and the Litany. By J. S. Blunt. *Third Edition.* Fcap. 8vo. 3s. 6d.

Confirmation. By J. S. Blunt, Author of "Readings on the Morning and Evening Prayer," &c. Fcap. 8vo. 3s. 6d.

Life after Confirmation. By the same Author. 18mo. 1s.

A History of the Church of England from the Accession of James II. to the Rise of the Bangorian Controversy in 1717. By the Rev. T. Debary, M.A. 8vo. 14s.

A Treatise on Metaphysics in Connection with Revealed Religion. By the Rev. J. H. MacMahon. 8vo. 14s.

Aids to Pastoral Visitation, selected and arranged by the Rev. H. B. Browning, M.A., Curate of St. George, Stamford. *Second Edition.* Fcap. 8vo. 3s. 6d.

Remarks on Certain Offices of the Church of England, popularly termed the Occasional Services. By the Rev. W. J. Dampier, 12mo. 5s.

The Sympathy of Christ. Six Readings for the Sundays in Lent, or for the Days of the Holy Week. By the Rev. W. J. Dampier, M.A., Vicar of Coggeshall. *Second Edition.* 18mo. 2s. 6d.

Reasons of Faith; or, the Order of the Christian Argument developed and explained. By the Rev. G. S. Drew, M.A. Fcap. 8vo. 4s. 6d.

Charles and Josiah; or, Friendly Conversations between a Churchman and a Quaker. Crown 8vo. 5s.

The English Churchman's Signal. By the Writer of "A Plain Word to the Wise in Heart." Fcap. 8vo. 2s. 6d.

A Plain Word to the Wise in Heart on our Duties at Church, and on our Prayer Book. *Fourth Edition.* Sewed, 1s. 6d.

The Book of Psalms (Prayer Book Version). With Short Headings and Explanatory Notes. By the Rev. Ernest Hawkins, B.D., Prebendary of St. Paul's. *Second and cheaper Edition, revised and enlarged,* Fcap. 8vo., cloth limp, red edges, 2s. 6d.

Family Prayers:—containing Psalms, Lessons, and Prayers, for every Morning and Evening in the Week. By the Rev. Ernest Hawkins, B.D., Prebendary of St. Paul's. *Eighth Edition.* Fcap. 8vo. 1s.; sewed, 9d.

Household Prayers on Scriptural Subjects, for Four Weeks. With Forms for various occasions. By a Member of the Church of England. *Second Edition, enlarged.* 8vo. 4s. 6d.

Forms of Prayer adapted to each Day of the Week. For use in Families or Households. By the Rev. John Jebb, D.D., 8vo. 2s. 6d.

Walton's Lives of Donne, Wotton, Hooker, Herbert, and Sanderson. A New Edition, to which is now added a Memoir of Mr. Isaac Walton, by William Dowling, Esq. of the Inner Temple, Barrister-at-Law. With Illustrative Notes, numerous Portraits, and other Engravings, Index, &c. Crown 8vo. 10s. 6d. Calf antique, 15s. Morocco, 18s.

The Life of Martin Luther. By H. Worsley, M. A., Rector of Easton, Suffolk. 2 vols. 8vo. 1l. 4s.

Papers on Preaching and Public Speaking. By a Wykehamist. Fcap. 8vo. 5s.

This volume is an enlargement and extension, with corrections, of the Papers which appeared in the " Guardian " in 1858-9.

The Speaker at Home. Chapters on Public Speaking and Reading aloud, by the Rev. J. J. Halcombe, M.A., and on the Physiology of Speech, by W. H. Stone, M.A., M.B. *Second Edition.* Fcap. 8vo. 3s. 6d.

Civilization considered as a Science in Relation to its Essence, its Elements, and its End. By George Harris, F.S.A., of the Middle Temple, Barrister at Law, Author of " The Life of Lord Chancellor Hardwicke." 8vo. 12s.

The Church Hymnal, (with or without Psalms.) 12mo. Large Type, 1s. 6d. 18mo. 1s. 32mo. for Parochial Schools, 6d.

This book is now in use in every English Diocese, and is the *Authorized* Book in some of the Colonial Dioceses.

Three Lectures on Archbishop Cranmer. By the Rev. C. J. Burton, M.A., Chancellor of Carlisle. 12mo. 3s.

Church Reading: according to the method advised by Thomas Sheridan. By the Rev. J. J. Halcombe, M.A. 8vo. 3s. 6d.

The Bishop of Worcester's Primary Charge, August, 1862. 8vo. 2s.

The Offertory : the most excellent way of contributing Money for Christian Purposes. By J. H. Markland, D.C.L., F.R.S., S.A. *Second Edition, enlarged*, 2d.

*** Messrs. Bell and Daldy are agents for the Publications of the Society for the Propagation of the Gospel in Foreign Parts.

BY THE REV. J. ERSKINE CLARKE, *of Derby.*

HEART Music, for the Hearth-Ring ; the Street-Walk ; the Country Stroll; the Work-Hours; the Rest-Day; the Trouble-Time. *New Edition.* 1s. paper; 1s. 6d. cloth limp.

The Giant's Arrows. A Book for the Children of Working People. 16mo. 6d.; cloth, 1s.

Children at Church. Twelve Simple Sermons. 2 vols. 1s. each ; 1s. 6d. cloth, gilt ; or together in 1 vol. cloth gilt, 2s. 6d.

Plain Papers on the Social Economy of the People. Fcap. 8vo. 2s. 6d.

No. 1. Recreations of the People.—No. 2. Penny Banks.—No. 3. Labourers' Clubs and Working Men's Refreshment Rooms.—No. 4. Children of the People. 6d. each.

The Devotional Library.

Edited by the Very Rev. W. F. Hook, D.D., Dean of Chichester.

A Series of Works, original or selected from well-known Church of England Divines, published at the lowest price, and suitable, from their practical character and cheapness, for Parochial distribution.

SHORT Meditations for Every Day in the Year. 2 vols. (1260 pages,) 32mo. Cloth, 5s.; calf, gilt edges, 9s. Calf antique, 12s.

In Separate Parts.

ADVENT to LENT, cloth, 1s.; limp calf, gilt edges, 2s. 6d.; LENT, cloth, 9d.; calf, 2s. 3d. EASTER, cloth, 9d.; calf, 2s. 3d. TRINITY, Part I. 1s.; calf, 2s. 6d. TRINITY, Part II. 1s.; calf, 2s. 6d.

*** *Large Paper Edition*, 4 vols. fcap. 8vo. large type. 14s. Morocco, 30s.

The Christian taught by the Church's Services. (490 pages), royal 32mo. Cloth, 2s. 6d.; calf, gilt edges, 4s. 6d. Calf antique, 6s.

In Separate Parts.

ADVENT TO TRINITY, cloth, 1s.; limp calf, gilt edges, 2s. 6d. TRINITY, cloth, 8d.; calf, 2s. 2d. MINOR FESTIVALS, 8d.; calf, 2s. 2d.

*** *Large Paper Edition*, Fcap. 8vo. large type. 6s. 6d. Calf antique, or morocco, 11s. 6d.

Devotions for Domestic Use. 32mo. cloth, 2s.; calf, gilt edges, 4s. Calf antique, 5s. 6d. Containing:—

The Common Prayer Book the best Companion in the Family as well as in the Temple. 3d.
Litanies for Domestic Use, 2d.
Family Prayers; or, Morning and Evening Services for every Day in the Week. By the Bishop of Salisbury; cloth, 6d.; calf, 2s.
Bishop Hall's Sacred Aphorisms. Selected and arranged with the Texts to which they refer. By the Rev. R. B. Exton, M.A.; cloth, 9d.

*** These are arranged together as being suitable for Domestic Use; but they may be had separately at the prices affixed.

Aids to a Holy Life. First Series. 32mo. Cloth, 1s. 6d.; calf, gilt edges, 3s. 6d. Calf antique, 5s. Containing:—

Prayers for the Young. By Dr. Hook, ½d.
Pastoral Address to a Young Communicant. By Dr. Hook, ½d.
Helps to Self-Examination. By W. F. Hook, D.D., ½d.
Directions for Spending One Day Well. By Archbishop Synge, ½d.
Rules for the Conduct of Human Life. By Archbishop Synge. 1d.
The Sum of Christianity, wherein a short and plain Account is given of the Christian Faith; Christian's Duty; Christian Prayer; Christian Sacrament. By C. Ellis, 1d.
Ejaculatory Prayer; or, the Duty of Offering up Short Prayers to God on all Occasions. By R. Cook. 2d.
Prayers for a Week. From J. Sorocold, 2d.
Companion to the Altar; being Prayers, Thanksgivings, and Meditations. Edited by Dr. Hook. Cloth, 6d.

*** Any of the above may be had for distribution at the prices affixed; they are arranged together as being suitable for Young Persons and for Private Devotion.

The Devotional Library continued.

Aids to a Holy Life. Second Series. 32mo. Cloth, 2s.; calf, gilt edges, 4s. Calf antique, 5s. 6d. Containing:—
Holy Thoughts and Prayers, arranged for Daily Use on each Day in the Week, 3d.
The Retired Christian exercised on Divine Thoughts and Heavenly Meditations. By Bishop Ken. 3d.
Penitential Reflections for the Holy Season of Lent, and other Days of Fasting and Abstinence during the Year. 6d.
The Crucified Jesus; a Devotional Commentary on the XXII and XXIII Chapters of St. Luke. By A. Horneck, D.D. 3d.
Short Reflections for every Morning and Evening during the Week. By N. Spinckes, 2d.
The Sick Man Visited; or, Meditations and Prayers for the Sick Room. By N. Spinckes, 3d.

*** These are arranged together as being suitable for Private Meditation and Prayer: they may be had separately at the prices affixed.

Helps to Daily Devotion. 32mo. Cloth, 8d. Containing:—
The Sum of Christianity, 1d.
Directions for spending One Day Well, ½d.
Helps to Self-Examination, ½d.
Short Reflections for Morning and Evening, 2d.
Prayers for a Week, 2d.

The History of our Lord and Saviour Jesus Christ; in Three Parts, with suitable Meditations and Prayers. By W. Reading, M.A. 32mo. Cloth, 2s.; calf, gilt edges, 4s. Calf antique, 5s. 6d.

Hall's Sacred Aphorisms. Selected and arranged with the Texts to which they refer, by the Rev. R. B. Exton, M.A. 32mo. cloth, 9d.; limp calf, gilt edges, 2s. 3d.

Devout Musings on the Book of Psalms. 2 vols. 32mo. Cloth, 5s.; calf, gilt edges, 9s.; calf antique, 12s. Or, in four parts, price 1s. each; limp calf, gilt edges, 2s. 6d.

The Church Sunday School Hymn Book. 32mo. cloth, 8d.; calf, gilt edges, 2s. 6d.

*** A *Large Paper Edition* for Prizes, &c. 1s. 6d.; calf, gilt edges, 3s. 6d.

SHORT Meditations for Every Day in the Year. Edited by the Very Rev. W. F. Hook, D.D. *New Edition.* 4 vols. fcap. 8vo., large type, 14s.; morocco, 30s.

The Christian taught by the Church's Services. Edited by the Very Rev. W. F. Hook, D.D. *New Edition*, fcap. 8vo. large type. 6s. 6d. Antique calf, or morocco, 11s. 6d.

Holy Thoughts and Prayers, arranged for Daily Use on each Day of the Week, according to the stated Hours of Prayer. *Fifth Edition*, with additions. 16mo. Cloth, red edges, 2s.; calf, gilt edges, 3s.

A Companion to the Altar. Being Prayers, Thanksgivings, and Meditations, and the Office of the Holy Communion. Edited by the Very Rev. W. F. Hook, D.D. *Second Edition.* Handsomely printed in red and black. 32mo. Cloth, red edges, 2s. Morocco, 3s. 6d.

The Church Sunday School Hymn Book. Edited by W. F. Hook, D.D. *Large paper.* Cloth, 1s. 6d.; calf, gilt edges, 3s. 6d.

*** For cheap editions of the above Five Books, see List of the Devotional Library.

EDUCATIONAL BOOKS.

Bibliotheca Classica.

A Series of Greek and Latin Authors. With English Notes. 8vo. Edited by various Scholars, under the direction of G Long, Esq., M.A., Classical Lecturer of Brighton College; and the late Rev. A. J. Macleane, M.A., Head Master of King Edward's School, Bath.

ÆSCHYLUS. By F. A. Paley, M.A. 18s.

Cicero's Orations. Edited by G. Long, M.A. 4 vols.
Vol. I. 16s.; Vol. II. 14s; Vol. III. 16s.; Vol. IV. 18s.

Demosthenes. By R. Whiston, M.A., Head Master of Rochester Grammar School. Vol. I. 16s. Vol. II. *preparing*.

Euripides. By F. A. Paley, M.A. 3 vols. 16s. each.

Herodotus. By J. W. Blakesley, B.D., late Fellow and Tutor of Trinity College, Cambridge. 2 vols. 32s.

Hesiod. By F. A. Paley, M.A. 10s. 6d.

Homer. By F. A. Paley, M. A. Vol. I. [*Preparing*.

Horace. By A. J. Macleane, M.A. 18s.

Juvenal and Persius. By A. J. Macleane, M.A. 14s.

Plato. By W. H. Thompson, M.A. Vol. I. [*Preparing*.

Sophocles. By F. H. Blaydes, M.A. Vol. I. 18s. Vol. II. *preparing*.

Terence. By E. St. J. Parry, M.A., Balliol College, Oxford. 18s.

Virgil. By J. Conington, M.A., Professor of Latin at Oxford. Vol. I. containing the Bucolics and Georgics. 12s. Vol. II. containing the Æneid, Books I. to VI. 14s. Vol. III. *preparing*.

Grammar=School Classics.

A Series of Greek and Latin Authors. Newly Edited, with English Notes for Schools. Fcap. 8vo.

CAESARIS Commentarii de Bello Gallico. *Second Edition*. By G. Long, M.A. 5s. 6d.

Caesar de Bello Gallico, Books 1 to 3. With English Notes for Junior Classes. By G. Long, M.A. 2s. 6d.

M. Tullii Ciceronis Cato Major, Sive de Senectute, Laelius, Sive de Amicitia, et Epistolae Selectae. By G. Long, M.A. 4s. 6d.

Quinti Horatii Flacci Opera Omnia. By A. J. Macleane, 6s. 6d.

Juvenalis Satirae XVI. By H. Prior, M.A. (Expurgated Edition.) 4s. 6d.

Grammar-School Classics continued.

P. Ovidii Nasonis Fastorum Libri Sex. By F. A. Paley. 5s.

C. Sallustii Crispi Catilina et Jugurtha. By G. Long, M.A. 5s.

Taciti Germania et Agricola. By P. Frost, M.A. 3s. 6d.

Xenophontis Anabasis, with Introduction; Geographical and other Notes, Itinerary, and Three Maps compiled from recent surveys. By J. F. Macmichael, B.A. *New Edition.* 5s.

Xenophontis Cyropaedia. By G. M. Gorham, M.A., late Fellow of Trinity College, Cambridge. 6s.

Uniform with the above.

The New Testament in Greek. With English Notes and Prefaces by J. F. Macmichael, B.A. 730 pages. 7s. 6d.

Cambridge Greek and Latin Texts.

THIS series is intended to supply for the use of Schools and Students cheap and accurate editions of the Classics, which shall be superior in mechanical execution to the small German editions now current in this country, and more convenient in form.

The texts of the *Bibliotheca Classica* and *Grammar School Classics*, so far as they have been published, will be adopted. These editions have taken their place amongst scholars as valuable contributions to the Classical Literature of this country, and are admitted to be good examples of the judicious and practical nature of English scholarship; and as the editors have formed their texts from a careful examination of the best editions extant, it is believed that no texts better for general use can be found.

The volumes will be well printed at the Cambridge University Press, in a 16mo. size, and will be issued at short intervals.

ÆSCHYLUS, ex novissima recensione F. A. Paley. 3s.

Cæsar de Bello Gallico, recensuit G. Long, A.M. 2s.

Cicero de Senectute et de Amicitia et Epistolæ Selectæ, recensuit G. Long, A.M. 1s. 6d.

Euripides, ex recensione F. A. Paley, A. M. 3 vols. 3s. 6d. each.

Herodotus, recensuit J. W. Blakesley, S.T.B. 2 vols. 7s.

Horatius, ex recensione A. J. Macleane, A.M. 2s. 6d.

Lucretius, recognovit H. A. J. Munro, A.M. 2s. 6d.

Sallusti Crispi Catilina et Jugurtha, recognovit G. Long, A.M. 1s. 6d.

Thucydides, recensuit J. G. Donaldson, S.T.P. 2 vols. 7s.

Vergilius, ex recensione J. Conington, A.M. 3s. 6d.

Xenophontis Anabasis recensuit J. F. Macmichael, A.B. 2s. 6d.

Novum Testamentum Graecum Textus Stephanici, 1550. Accedunt variae Lectiones editionum Bezae, Elzeviri, Lachmanni, Tischendorfii. Tregellesii, curante F. H. Scrivener, A.M. 4s. 6d.

Also, on 4to. writing paper, for MSS. notes. Half bound, gilt top, 12s.

Foreign Classics.

With English Notes for Schools. Uniform with the GRAMMAR SCHOOL CLASSICS. Fcap. 8vo.

GERMAN Ballads from Uhland, Goethe, and Schiller, with Introductions to each Poem, copious Explanatory Notes, and Biographical Notices. Edited by C. L. Bielefeld. 3s. 6d.

Schiller's Wallenstein, complete Text. Edited by Dr. A. Buchheim. 6s 6d.

Picciola, by X. B. Saintine. Edited by Dr. Dubuc. *Second Edition, revised.* 3s. 6d.

This interesting story has been selected with the intention of providing for schools and young persons a good specimen of contemporary French literature, free from the solecisms which are frequently met with in writers of a past age.

Select Fables of La Fontaine. *Third Edition, revised.* Edited by F. Gase, M.A. 3s.

"None need now be afraid to introduce this eminently French author, either on account of the difficulty of translating him, or the occasional licence of thought and expression in which he indulges. The renderings of idiomatic passages are unusually good, and the purity of English perfect."—*Athenæum.*

Histoire de Charles XII. par Voltaire. Edited by L. Direy. *Third Edition, revised.* 3s. 6d.

Aventures de Télémaque, par Fénélon. Edited by C. J. Delille. *Second Edition, revised.* 4s. 6d.

Classical Tables. 8vo.

NOTABILIA Quædam : or, the principal tenses of such Irregular Greek Verbs and such elementary Greek, Latin, and French Constructions as are of constant occurrence. 1s. 6d.

Greek Accidence. By the Rev. P. Frost, M. A. 1s.

Latin Accidence. By the Rev. P. Frost, M. A. 1s.

Latin Versification. 1s.

The Principles of Latin Syntax. 1s.

Homeric Dialect: its leading Forms and Peculiarities. By J. S. Baird, T.C.D. 1s. 6d.

A Catalogue of Greek Verbs, Irregular and Defective; their leading formations, tenses in use, and dialectic inflexions; with a copious Appendix, containing Paradigms for conjugation, Rules for formation of tenses, &c. &c. By J. S. Baird, T.C.D. *New Edition, revised.* 3s. 6d.

Richmond Rules to form the Ovidian Distich, &c. By J. Tate, M.A. *New Edition, revised.* 1s. 6d.

AN Atlas of Classical Geography, containing 24 Maps; constructed by W. Hughes, and edited by G. Long. *New Edition,* with coloured outlines, and an Index of Places. 12s. 6d.

A Grammar School Atlas of Classical Geography. The Maps constructed by W. Hughes, and edited by G. Long. Imp. 8vo. 5s.

First Classical Maps, with Chronological Tables of Grecian and Roman History, Tables of Jewish Chronology, and a Map of Palestine. By the Rev. J. Tate, M.A. *Third Edition.* Imp. 8vo. 7s. 6d.

Analecta Graeca Minora. With Introductory Sentences, English Notes, and a Dictionary. By the Rev. P. Frost, late Fellow of St. John's College, Cambridge. Fcap. 8vo. 3s. 6d.

Materials for Greek Prose Composition. By the Rev. P. Frost, M.A. Fcap. 8vo. 3s. 6d. Key, 5s.

Materials for Latin Prose Composition. By the Rev. P. Frost, M.A. *Third Edition.* 12mo. 2s. 6d. Key, 4s.

The Choephorae of Æschylus and Scholia. Revised and interpreted by J. F. Davies, Esq., B.A., Trin. Coll., Dublin. 8vo. 7s. 6d.

Auxilia Graeca: containing Forms of Parsing and Greek Trees, the Greek Prepositions, Rules of Accentuation, Greek Idioms, &c. &c. By the Rev. H. Fowler, M.A. 12mo. 3s. 6d.

Homer and English Metre. An Essay on the Translating of the Iliad and Odyssey. With a Literal Rendering in the Spenserian Stanza of the First Book of the Odyssey, and Specimens of the Iliad. By William G. T. Barter, Esq., Author of " A Literal Translation, in Spenserian Stanza, of the Iliad of Homer." Crown 8vo. 6s. 6d.

A Latin Grammar. By T. Hewitt Key, M.A., F.R.S., Professor of Comparative Grammar, and Head Master of the Junior School, in University College. *Third Edition, revised.* Post 8vo. 8s.

A Short Latin Grammar, for Schools. By T. H. Key, M.A., F.R.S. *Third Edition.* Post 8vo. 3s. 6d.

Latin Accidence. Consisting of the Forms, and intended to prepare boys for Key's Short Latin Grammar. Post 8vo. 2s.

A First Cheque Book for Latin Verse Makers. By the Rev. F. Gretton, Stamford Free Grammar School. 1s. 6d. Key, 2s. 6d.

Reddenda; or Passages with Parallel Hints for translation into Latin Prose and Verse. By the Rev. F. E. Gretton. Crown 8vo. 4s. 6d.

Rules for the Genders of Latin Nouns, and the Perfects and Supines of Verbs: with hints on Construing, &c. By H. Haines, M.A. 1s. 6d.

Latin Prose Lessons. By the Rev. A. Church, M.A., one of the Masters of Merchant Taylors' School. Fcap. 8vo. 2s. 6d.

The Works of Virgil, closely rendered into English Rhythm, and illustrated from British Poets of the 16th, 17th, and 18th Centuries. By the Rev. R. C. Singleton, M.A. 2 vols. post 8vo. 18s.

Quintus Horatius Flaccus. Illustrated with 50 Engravings from the Antique. Fcap. 8vo. 5s. Morocco, 9s.

Selections from Ovid: Amores, Tristia, Heroides, Metamorphoses. With English Notes, by the Rev. A. J. Macleane, M.A. Fcap. 8vo. 3s. 6d.

Sabrinae Corolla in hortulis Regiae Scholae Salopiensis contexuerunt tres viri floribus legendis. *Editio Altera.* 8vo. 12s. Morocco, 21s.

Dual Arithmetic, a New Art, by Oliver Byrne, formerly Professor of Mathematics at the late College of Civil Engineers, Putney. 8vo. 10s. 6d.

A Graduated Series of Exercises in Elementary Algebra, with an Appendix containing Miscellaneous Examples. By the Rev. G. F. Wright, M.A., Mathematical Master at Wellington College. Crown 8vo. 3s. 6d.

The Elements of Euclid. Books I.—VI. XI. 1—21; XII. 1, 2; a new text, based on that of Simson, with Exercises. Edited by H. J. Hose, late Mathematical Master of Westminster School. Fcap. 4s. 6d.

Educational Books. 27

A Graduated Series of Exercises on the Elements of Euclid: Books I.—VI.; XI. 1—21; XII. 1, 2. Selected and arranged by Henry J. Hose, M.A. 12mo. 1s.

The Enunciations and Figures belonging to the Propositions in the First Six and part of the Eleventh Books of Euclid's Elements, (usually read in the Universities,) prepared for Students in Geometry. By the Rev. J. Brasse, D.D. *New Edition.* Fcap. 8vo. 1s. On cards, in case, 5s. 6d.; without the Figures, 6d.

A Compendium of Facts and Formulæ in Pure and Mixed Mathematics. For the use of Mathematical Students. By G. R. Smalley, B.A., F.R.A.S. Fcap. 8vo. 3s. 6d.

A Table of Anti-Logarithms; containing to seven places of decimals, natural numbers, answering to all Logarithms from ·00001 to ·99999; and an improved table of Gauss' Logarithms, by which may be found the Logarithm of the sum or difference of two quantities. With an Appendix, containing a Table of Annuities for three Joint Lives at 3 per cent. Carlisle. By H. E. Filipowski. *Third Edition.* 8vo. 15s.

Handbook of the Slide Rule: showing its applicability to Arithmetic, including Interest and Annuities; Mensuration, including Land Surveying. With numerous Examples and useful Tables. By W. H. Bayley, H. M. East India Civil Service. 12mo. 6s.

The Mechanics of Construction; including the Theories on the Strength of Materials, Roofs, Arches, and Suspension Bridges. With numerous Examples. By Stephen Fenwick, Esq., of the Royal Military Academy, Woolwich. 8vo. 12s.

A NEW FRENCH COURSE, BY MONS. F. E. A. GASC, M.A.

FIRST French Book; being a New, Practical, and Easy Method of Learning the Elements of the French Language. *New Edition.* Fcap. 8vo. 1s. 6d.

French Fables, for Beginners, in Prose, with an Index of all the words at the end of the work. *New Edition.* Fcap. 8vo. 2s.

Second French Book; being a Grammar and Exercise Book, on a new and practical plan, and intended as a sequel to the "First French Book." *New Edition.* Fcap. 8vo. 2s. 6d.

A Key to the First and Second French Books. Fcap. 8vo. 3s. 6d.

Histoires Amusantes et Instructives; or, Selections of Complete Stories from the best French Modern Authors who have written for the Young. With English Notes. *New Edition.* Fcap. 8vo. 2s. 6d.

Practical Guide to Modern French Conversation: containing:—I. The most current and useful Phrases in Every-Day Talk; II. Everybody's Necessary Questions and Answers in Travel-Talk. *New Edition.* Fcap. 2s. 6d.

French Poetry for the Young. With English Notes, and preceded by a few plain Rules of French Prosody. Fcap. 8vo. 2s.

Materials for French Prose Composition; or, Selections from the best English Prose Writers. With copious Foot Notes, and Hints for Idiomatic Renderings. *New Edition.* Fcap. 8vo. 4s. 6d. Key, 6s.

Prosateurs Contemporains: or Selections in Prose, chiefly from contemporary French Literature. With English Notes. Fcap. 8vo. 5s.

Le Petit Compagnon: a French Talk-book for Little Children. With 52 Illustrations. 16mo. 2s. 6d.

THE French Drama; being a Selection of the best Tragedies and Comedies of Molière, Racine, P. Corneille, T. Corneille, and Voltaire. With Arguments in English at the head of each scene, and Notes, Critical and Explanatory, by A. Gombert. 18mo. Sold separately at 1s. each. Half-bound, 1s. 6d. each.

COMEDIES BY MOLIERE.

Le Misanthrope.
L'Avare.
Le Bourgeois Gentilhomme.
Le Tartuffe.
Le Malade Imaginaire.
Les Femmes Savantes.
Les Fourberies de Scapin.

Les Précieuses Ridicules.
L'Ecole des Femmes.
L'Ecole des Maris.
Le Médecin Malgré Lui.
M. de Pourceaugnac.
Amphitryon.

TRAGEDIES, &c. BY RACINE.

La Thébaïde, ou les Frères Ennemis.
Alexandre le Grand.
Andromaque.
Les Plaideurs, (Com.)
Britannicus.
Bérénice.

Bajazet.
Mithridate.
Iphigénie.
Phèdre.
Esther.
Athalie.

TRAGEDIES, &c. BY P. CORNEILLE.

Le Cid.
Horace.
Cinna.
Polyeucte.

Pompée.

BY T. CORNEILLE.
Ariane.

PLAYS BY VOLTAIRE.

Brutus.
Zaire.
Alzire.
Orestes.

Le Fanatisme.
Mérope.
La Mort de César.
Semiramis.

Le Nouveau Trésor: or, French Student's Companion: designed to facilitate the Translation of English into French at Sight. *Fifteenth Edition*, with Additions. By M. E*** S*****. 12mo. Roan, 3s. 6d.

A Test-Book for Students: Examination Papers for Students preparing for the Universities or for Appointments in the Army and Civil Service, and arranged for General Use in Schools. By the Rev. Thomas Stantial, M.A., Head Master of the Grammar School, Bridgwater. Part I.—History and Geography. 2s. 6d. Part II.—Language and Literature. 2s. 6d. Part III.—Mathematical Science. 2s. 6d. Part IV.—Physical Science. 1s. 6d. Or in 1 vol., Crown 8vo., 7s. 6d.

Tables of Comparative Chronology, illustrating the division of Universal History into Ancient, Mediæval, and Modern History; and containing a System of Combinations, distinguished by a particular type, to assist the Memory in retaining Dates. By W. E. Bickmore and the Rev. C. Bickmore, M.A. *Third Edition*. 4to. 5s.

A Course of Historical and Chronological Instruction. By W. E. Bickmore. 2 Parts. 12mo. 3s. 6d. each.

A Practical Synopsis of English History: or, A General Summary of Dates and Events for the use of Schools, Families, and Candidates for Public Examinations. By Arthur Bowes. *Fourth Edition*. 8vo. 2s.

Educational Books. 29

Under Government: an Official Key to the Civil Service, and Guide for Candidates seeking Appointments under the Crown. By J. C. Parkinson, Inland Revenue, Somerset House. *Third Edition.* Cr. 8vo. 3s. 6d.

Government Examinations; being a Companion to "Under Government," and a Guide to the Civil Service Examinations. By J. C. Parkinson. Crown 8vo. 2s. 6d.

The Student's Text-Book of English and General History, from B. C. 100 to the present time. With Genealogical Tables, and a Sketch of the English Constitution. By D. Beale. *Sixth Edition.* Post 8vo. Sewed, 2s. Cloth, 2s. 6d.
"This is very much in advance of most works we have seen devoted to similar purposes. We can award very high praise to a volume which may prove invaluable to teachers and taught."—*Athenæum.*

The Elements of the English Language for Schools and Colleges. By Ernest Adams, Ph. D. University College School. *New Edition, enlarged, and improved.* Crown 8vo. 4s. 6d.

The Geographical Text-Book; a Practical Geography, calculated to facilitate the study of that useful science, by a constant reference to the Blank Maps. By M. E ... S ..... *Second Edition.* 12mo. 2s.
II. The Blank Maps done up separately. 4to. 2s. coloured.

The Manual of Book-keeping; by an Experienced Clerk. 12mo. *Eighth Edition.* 4s.

Double Entry Elucidated. By B. W. Foster. *Eighth Edition.* 4to. 8s. 6d.

Penmanship, Theoretical and Practical, Illustrated and Explained. By B. F. Foster. 12mo. *New Edition.* 2s. 6d.

Goldsmith's (J.) Copy Books: five sorts, large, text, round, small, and mixed. Post 4to. on fine paper. 6s. per dozen.

The Young Ladies' School Record: or, Register of Studies and conduct. 12mo. 6d.

Welchman on the Thirty-nine Articles of the Church of England, with Scriptural Proofs, &c. 18mo. 2s. or interleaved for Students, 3s.

Bishop Jewel's Apology for the Church of England, with his famous Epistle on the Council of Trent, and a Memoir. 32mo. 2s.

A Short Explanation of the Epistles and Gospels of the Christian Year, with Questions for Schools. Royal 32mo. 2s. 6d.; calf, 4s. 6d.

Manual of Astronomy: a Popular Treatise on Descriptive, Physical, and Practical Astronomy. By John Drew, F.R.A.S. *Second Edition.* Fcap. 8vo. 5s.

The First Book of Botany. Being a Plain and Brief Introduction to that Science for Schools and Young Persons. By Mrs. Loudon. Illustrated with 36 Wood Engravings. *Second Edition.* 18mo. 1s.

English Poetry for Classical Schools; or, Florilegium Poeticum Anglicanum. 12mo. 1s. 6d.

BELL AND DALDY'S ILLUSTRATED SCHOOL BOOKS.
Royal 16mo.

SCHOOL Primer. 6d.

School Reader. [*Shortly.*

Poetry Book for Schools. 1s.

Old Testament History, in Simple Language. By the Rev. J. G. Wood, M.A. 1s. [*Ready.*

New Testament History, in Simple Language. By the Rev. J. G. Wood, M.A. [*Shortly.*

COURSE OF INSTRUCTION FOR THE YOUNG, BY HORACE GRANT.

EXERCISES for the Improvement of the Senses; for Young Children. 18mo. 1s. 6d.

Geography for Young Children. *New Edition.* 18mo. 2s.

Arithmetic for Young Children. *New Edition.* 18mo. 1s. 6d.

Arithmetic. Second Stage. *New Edition.* 18mo. 3s.

PERIODICALS.

THE Parish Magazine. Edited by J. Erskine Clarke, M.A., Derby. Monthly, price 1d. Volumes for 1859, 1860, 1861, and 1862, 1s. 6d. and 2s. each.

The Mission Field: a Monthly Record of the Proceedings of the Society for the Propagation of the Gospel. Vols. II. to VII. post 8vo. 3s. each. (Vol. I. is out of print.) Continued in Numbers, 2d. each.

The Gospel Missionary. Published for the Society for the Propagation of the Gospel in Foreign Parts, Monthly at ½d. Vols. II. to XII. in cloth, 1s. each. (Vol. I. is out of print.)

Missions to the Heathen; being Records of the Progress of the Efforts made by the Society for the Propagation of the Gospel in Foreign Parts for the Conversion of the Heathen. Published occasionally in a cheap form for distribution, at prices varying from 1d. to 1s. 6d. each. Nos. 1 to 43 are already published.

Church in the Colonies, consisting chiefly of Journals by the Colonial Bishops of their Progress and Special Visitations. Published occasionally at prices varying from 2d. to 1s. 6d. each. Nos. 1 to 37 are already published.

CLARKE'S COMMERCIAL COPY-BOOKS.
Price 4d. A liberal allowance to Schools and Colleges.

The FIRST COPY-BOOK contains *elementary turns*, with a broad mark like a T, which divides a well-formed turn into two equal parts. This exercise enables the learner to judge of *form, distance, and proportion.*

The SECOND contains *large-hand letters*, and the means by which such letters may be properly combined; the joinings in writing being probably as difficult to learn as the form of each character. This book also gives the whole alphabet, not in separate letters, but rather as one *word;* and, at the end of the alphabet, the difficult letters are repeated so as to render the writing of the pupil more thorough and *uniform.*

The THIRD contains additional *large-hand practice.*

The FOURTH contains *large-hand words*, commencing with *unflourished* capitals; and the words being short, the capitals in question receive the attention they demand. As Large, and Extra Large-text, to which the fingers of the learner are not equal, have been dispensed with in this series, the popular objection of having *too many Copy-books* for the pupil to drudge through, is now fairly met. When letters are very large, the scholar cannot compass them without stopping to change the position of his hand, which *destroys* the *freedom* which such writing is intended to promote.

The FIFTH contains the essentials of a useful kind of *small-hand*. There are first, as in large-hand, five easy letters of the alphabet, forming four copies, which of course are repeated. Then follows the remainder of the alphabet, with the difficult characters alluded to. The letters in this hand, especially the *a, c, d, g, o,* and *q*, are so formed that when the learner will have to correspond, his writing will not appear stiff. The copies in this book are not *mere Large-hand reduced.*

The SIXTH contains *small-hand copies*, with instructions as to the manner in which the pupil should hold his pen, so that when he leaves school he may not merely have some facility in copying, but really possess the information on the subject of writing which he may need at any future time.

The SEVENTH contains the foundation for a style of *small-hand*, adapted to females, *moderately pointed.*

The EIGHTH contains copies for females; and the holding of the pen is, of course, the subject to which they specially relate.

This Series is specially adapted for those who are preparing for a commercial life. It is generally found when a boy leaves school that his writing is of such a character that it is some months before it is available for book-keeping or accounts. The special object of this Series of Copy-Books is to form his writing in such a style that he may be put to the work of a counting-house at once. By following this course from the first the writing is kept free and legible, whilst it avoids unnecessary flourishing.

Specimens of hand-writing after a short course may be seen on application to the Publishers.

BELL AND DALDY'S
POCKET VOLUMES.
A SERIES OF SELECT WORKS OF FAVOURITE AUTHORS.

HE intention of the Publishers is to produce a Series of Volumes adapted for general reading, moderate in price, compact and elegant in form, and executed in a style fitting them to be permanently preserved.

They do not profess to compete with the so-called cheap volumes. They believe that a cheapness which is attained by the use of inferior type and paper, and absence of editorial care, and which results in volumes that no one cares to keep, is a false cheapness. They desire rather to produce books superior in quality, and relatively as cheap.

Each volume will be carefully revised by a competent editor, and printed at the Chiswick Press, on fine paper, with new type, and ornaments and initial letters specially designed for the series.

The *Pocket Volumes* will include all classes of Literature, both copyright and non-copyright;—Biography, History, Voyages, Travels, Poetry, sacred and secular, Books of Adventure and Fiction. They will include Translations of Foreign Books, and also such American Literature as may be considered worthy of adoption.

The Publishers desire to respect the moral claims of authors who cannot secure legal copyright in this country, and to remunerate equitably those whose works they may reprint.

The books will be issued at short intervals, in paper covers, at various prices, from 1s. to 3s. 6d., and in cloth, top edge gilt, at 6d. per volume extra, in half morocco, Roxburgh style, at 1s. extra, in antique or best plain morocco (Hayday), at 4s. extra.

Now Ready.

Burns's Poems. 2s. 6d.
Burns's Songs. 2s. 6d.
Walton's Complete Angler. Illustrated. 2s. 6d.
Sea Songs and Ballads. By Charles Dibdin, and others. 2s. 6d.
White's Natural History of Selborne. 3s.
Coleridge's Poems. 2s. 6d.
The Robin Hood Ballads. 2s. 6d.
The Midshipman. By Capt. Basil Hall, R.N. 3s.
The Lieutenant and Commander. By the same Author. 3s.
Southey's Life of Nelson. 2s. 6d.
Longfellow's Poems. 2s. 6d.

Lamb's Tales from Shakspeare. 2s. 6d.
Milton's Paradise Lost. 2s. 6d.
George Herbert's Poems. 2s.
George Herbert's Works. 3s.
Milton's Paradise Regained and other Poems. 2s. 6d.

Preparing.

Walton's Lives of Donne, Wotton, Hooker, &c.
The Conquest of India. By Capt. Basil Hall, R.N.
Gray's Poems.
Goldsmith's Poems.
Goldsmith's Vicar of Wakefield.
Henry Vaughan's Poems.
And others.

CHISWICK PRESS:—PRINTED BY WHITTINGHAM AND WILKINS,
TOOKS COURT, CHANCERY LANE.

www.ingramcontent.com/pod-product-compliance
Lightning Source LLC
Chambersburg PA
CBHW020157170426
43199CB00010B/1080